CARNIVAL OF SHAME
REFLECTIONS
ON THE CONSERVATIVE FIFTY-YEAR
BETRAYAL OF AMERICA

Let
Freedom
Ring

CARNIVAL OF SHAME
REFLECTIONS
ON THE CONSERVATIVE FIFTY-YEAR BETRAYAL OF AMERICA

M.G. MONTPELIER

To order additional copies of this book, contact:
Xlibris
844-714-8691
www.Xlibris.com
Orders@Xlibris.com
857296

ACKNOWLEDGEMENTS

I am indebted to so many who have pursued the truth of freedom betrayed, especially Charles Derber, Thom Hartmann, Chris Hedges, Nancy MacLean, Hedrick Smith, and Richard Wolff - to name just a few. To Casey Maddock, a special note of gratitude for her political acumen and editorial skills in bringing this project together. And to Professor Charles Derber, thank you, for so many invaluable insights into the making of the Republican "survival of the fittest" America, and so kindly allowing me to use for the "Ruling High Table" language from his book with Yale Magrass, *The Surplus American*. The political thoughts, comments, and opinions expressed in this work are mine unless otherwise noted.

September 3, 1783

UNITED STATES CONSTITUTION

Preamble: We the People of the United States, in Order to form a more perfect Union, establish Justice, insure domestic Tranquility, provide for the common defense, promote the general Welfare, and secure the Blessings of Liberty to ourselves and our Posterity, do ordain and establish this Constitution for the United States of America.

XIV Amendment: Section1. All persons born or naturalized… are citizens of the United States and the State wherein they reside. No State shall make or enforce any law which shall abridge the privileges or immunities of citizens of the United States.

XIV Amendment: Section 3. No person shall be a Senator or Representative…or hold any office…having previously taken an oath…to support the Constitution of the United States…[who] shall have been engaged in insurrection or rebellion against same, or given aid or comfort to the enemies thereof.

XV Amendment: Section 1. The right of citizens of the United States to vote shall not be denied or abridged by the United States or by any State on account of race, color or previous condition of servitude.

LEST WE FORGET

Remember we must
They came promising
"Trickle-Down" Prosperity
Then
Repealed the rule of law
Took our jobs and pensions
Undermined our civil liberties
And
Freedom was no more
Greed enveloped the land
Corruption reigned supreme
As
Fascism Triumphed in
The Suffering Silence
Of Human Bondage

CONTENTS

SENSELESS MISERY

I see far and near the senseless
Misery of corruption, Political
Betrayal, and Racial Injustice

I bear the pain of an abandoned
Surplus people politically deceived,
Disenfranchised and Forgotten

I behold the hopelessness of a
Desperate mother's despair, the
Chains of the mass incarcerated

I share the inner quiet of a long
Suffering people longing for
Liberty, Truth, and Justice

PREFACE

*"Behind the ostensible
government sits enthroned
an invisible government
owing no allegiance
and acknowledging no
responsibility to the people."*
**President
Theodore Roosevelt**

Carnival of Shame is a compendium of my previously published works on the Conservative Fifty-Year Republican "Assault on America," from the 1971 "Powell" strategic grand design to "save capitalism from democracy" and the 1981 Republican "Trickle-Down" Revolution to the January 6, 2021 violent "maga" insurrection to overturn the Constitution and the electoral will of the people.

The narrative is a reflective commentary coupled with facts from the historical record on the political-economic reality of America's dysfunctional "dark money" politics in today's Conservative Orwellian world of lies, deception, and deceit. My views focus on today's reality that we are a People of Liberty politically and economically abandoned as just "surplus" struggling to survive in a Republican wasteland of concentrated wealth, ideological extremism, hypocrisy and betrayal.

To every working American struggling to make ends meet, it is an APPEAL for political redress in the battle to overcome the Conservative "survival of the fittest" politics in today's Republican world of "Trickle-Down" human bondage. It is a PLEA for a Citizen Electoral Mandate to END the Republican political-economic predatory culture of injustice, poverty, and death.

For me and the generation of 1945 to 1975, we were once a middle class people prosperous and secure. That was before the 1971 Republican "grand design" to "save capitalism from democracy" and the making of the Conservative financialized "Trickle-Down" debt-based economy. Then, every American shared in some way the good times of America's Industrial Golden Age. We were a hard working industrious people, stable and strong, with a progressive living wage, an affordable mortgage, medical care, and education, and the promise of a dignified retirement in old age.

But, not to be forgotten, it was also a grand moment of the American experience, as we, a People of Liberty, pledged unequivocally our sacred honor to defend the "Constitution of the United States" against all enemies "foreign and domestic," and "national interest" meant, in real tangible terms, safeguarding the "general welfare" of a free democratic people.

After five decades of the Republican "Pooring of America," that once middle class affluence is now a "Trickle-Down" subsistence-wage, debt-based casino society of concentrated wealth. America in every sector of American life is a Republican political-economic autocracy of monopoly supremacy, subsistence-wages, financial growth gimmicks, speculation schemes, and the destructive hedge fund pillaging of America's infrastructure. And as a result, we are a people consigned to endure today's Republican "surplus left behind" America of *every man for himself* struggling to secure the basic necessities of life.

With the onset of the 1971 Powell grand design to "save capitalism from democracy," the rise and impact of the Business Roundtable, Heritage Foundation, and Federalist Society, coupled with a Conservative politicized Supreme Court's legalization of unlimited, unaccountable, Ultra-Rich political "dark money," America's electoral campaign integrity and democratic institutions have gradually become undermined and compromised. The historical perspective today suggests that the deaths of President

Kennedy in 1963 and Martin Luther King, Jr. in 1968, were not only to be the demise of an envisioned "new frontier" of the people and a beginning of a new era of "equality" in America, but the opening round of dark money "white power" conspiracies in the coming political-economic transformation of democracy in America.

The ruthless, fanatical, Republican decade's assault on America's People of Liberty is today the social-economic reality of the Conservative "big money" vested interest Republican "Trickle-Down" political agenda. Whether or not we are willing to admit the truth to ourselves, we are a struggling democratic people mercilessly abandoned to the greed, corruption, and injustice of the Conservative "deregulated" predatory "Trickle-Down" subsistence economy. We are a people in a life struggle not only for the welfare of our families and our children's future, but what's to come for of a disenfranchised hijacked "maga" America.

In these desperate and perilous times we bear witness to the plight of millions of suffering Americans sacrificed and abandoned as just "surplus" unworthies to the ravages of the "Trickle-Down" Conservatism of *you're on your own* desperation. *"What a weary time," Charles Bukowski laments, "to have the desire and the need to live but not the ability."*

The time is now that we keep in mind as a People of Liberty the warning of Daniel Webster to America: *"Our destruction should it come…will be from the inattention of the people to the concerns of their government…falling prey to the dupes of designing men and become the instruments of their own undoing".*

We are in this American moment a politically polarized divided nation given to Republican lies, false narratives, legislative chaos, extreme gun violence, and "white supremacy" politics. Considering the political extremism of the Republican controlled "House" of "maga" seditionists, the unlimited campaign "dark money" of the financial power elite, and Republican voter district gerrymandering and voter suppression laws, we can expect the coming election will be exposed to every Conservative political resource of political extremism. Without question the Conservative "maga" establishment will make every effort to "burn or rule" in a grand finale "Assault on Democracy" to seize absolute political power in 2024.

Now as we approach the Conservative "apocalyptic" reality of 2024, we must appreciate that 2024 is not just another election. This is America's electoral moment where the future of Democracy, Freedom, and Justice in America is up for grabs. Every ballot cast in 2024, is a ballot for one issue, and one issue only: **"POWER!" - the "power" to preserve or destroy "democracy in America for all generations to come.**

For a reminder of what a Republican power grab in 2024 would bring to America, imagine for a moment the tyranny and horror of Republican authoritarian rule over a "lawless" racist America of anger, hate, and chaos, unfettered predatory capitalism, and the terror of unbridled forever present gun violence on the streets of America

Presently, the 2024 Republican Machiavellian "maga" frontrunner, a twice impeached, four-time criminally indicted insurrectionist, is being unequivocally upfront in laying out the Orwellian "maga" political supremacy agenda for restructuring American democracy into a corrupt political authoritarian order. Appreciate we must a "maga" power grab for what it portends: (1) a promise of dictatorship on day one (2) dismantling of the democratic process (3) removal by "executive order" of "birth right" citizenship; (4) rollback of America's "civil rights" laws, (5) replacement of "civil servants" in mass with political loyalists, (6) work camps for the politically designated "vermin" and "rabble" of "maga" retribution, and (7) employment of active military units against civil demonstrations.

This is the Republican plan for a Conservative "maga" America on the assumption of power: a 1930s racist authoritarian model of "fascism" for a 2025 America.

BELIEVE HIM! This will be the people's "forever reality" in a Republican "maga" authoritarian political world.

The moment is here we come together as a free democratic people for an America of secure democratic institutions, a strong middle class, stable living-wage jobs, and a prosperous America of "Liberty and Justice for All."

It is my hope *Carnival of Shame* will be a wakeup call for real grass roots democracy in 2024. The outcome of this struggle is nothing less than Freedom itself; Freedom for a people of Democracy, Truth, and Justice liberated from the Republican Corruption and Injustice of the political-economic Greed of the Conservative "laissez-faire" Profit over People "survival of the fittest" world of "individual extremism."

M.G. Montpelier
December 27, 2023

FREEDOM LOST

To Be DOWNTRODDEN
Subjugated and Exploited
IS NOT FREEDOM!

To Be IMPOVERISHED
Desperate and Hopeless
IS NOT FREEDOM!

To Be MARGINALIZED
Rejected and Scorned
IS NOT FREEDOM!

To Be SURPLUS
Abandoned and Alone
IS NOT FREEDOM!

PROLOGUE

With
President
Franklin Roosevelt

ON

FREE ENTERPRISE

"True individual freedom cannot exist without economic security and independence...Freedom means the supremacy of human rights everywhere. Our support goes to those who struggle to gain those rights and keep them. Our strength is our unity of purpose."

"Unhappy events abroad have taught us two simple truths about the liberty of a democratic people. The FIRST TRUTH is that the liberty of a democracy is not safe if the people tolerate the growth of private power to a point where it becomes stronger than the democratic itself. That, in its essence, is Fascism – ownership of Government by an individual, by a group, or by any other controlling private power. The SECOND TRUTH is that the liberty of a democracy is not safe if its business system does not provide employment and produce and distribute goods in such a way as to sustain an accepted standard of living.

Among us today a concentration of private power without equal in history is growing. This concentration is seriously impairing the economic effectiveness of private enterprise as a way of providing employment for labor and capital and as a way of assuring a more equitable distribution of income and earnings among the people of the nation as a whole... Of all the corporations reporting, less than 5per cent of them owned 87 per cent of all the assets of all of them...less than 4 per cent of them earned 84 per cent of all the net profits of all of them. In 1929 [before the crash] three-tenths of 1 per cent of our population received 78 per cent of the dividends...

We believe in a way of living in which political democracy and free enterprise for profit should serve to protect each other – to ensure a maximum of human liberty not for a few but for all ... Today's answer on the part of the average man and woman...is that if there is a danger it comes from that concentrated private economic power which is struggling so hard to master our democratic government.

Private enterprise is ceasing to be free enterprise and is becoming a cluster of private collectivisms: masking as a system of free enterprise after the American model... in fact becoming a concealed cartel system... We all want efficient industrial growth and the advantages of mass production [that] has evolved into banker control of industry. We oppose that. Interlocking financial controls have taken from American business much of its traditional virility, independence, adaptability and daring – without compensating advantages. They have not given the stability they promised.

One of the primary causes of our present difficulties, in the disappearance of price competition in many industrial fields ... When prices are privately managed at levels above those which would be determined by free competition, everybody pays...price controls interfere with the ability of free enterprise to fill the needs of the community and provide employment for capital and labor... If free enterprise is left to its own devices...as it is today, it obviously cannot adjust itself to meet the needs and the demands of the country… monopolistic controls which each business group imposes for its own benefit, inevitability destroys the buying power of the nations as a whole.

It is of course necessary to operate the competitive system of free enterprise intelligently… Examination of methods of conducting and controlling private enterprise which keep it from furnishing jobs or income or opportunity…is long overdue… No people, least of all a democratic people, will be content to go to work or to accept some standard of living which obviously and woefully falls short of their capacity to produce. No people, least of all a people with our traditions of personal liberty, will endure the slow erosion of opportunity for the common man, the oppressive sense of helplessness under the domination of a few, which are overshadowing our whole economic life.

The power of a few to manage the economic life of the nation must be diffused among the many or be transferred to the public and its democratically responsible government. If prices are to be managed and administered, if the nation's business is to be allotted by plan and not by competition, that power should not be vested in any private group or cartel… We must find practical controls over blind economic forces as well as overly blindly selfish men. Government can deal and should deal with blindly selfish men… I recommend that Congress [enact legislation to] effectively control the operation of bank holding companies [and] that this legislation make provision for the gradual separation of banks from holding company control or ownership… Business monopoly in America paralyses the system of free enterprise…and is fatal to those who manipulate it."

Franklin Roosevelt
Message to Congress
April 29, 1938

LEFT TO DIE

Across America
A Surplus People
"Left to Die"
Struggle to survive
Conservative "Trickle-Down"
Greed and Corruption

Across America
A Surplus People
Subsist
On Conservative"
"Trickle-Down"
Want and Desperation

Across America
A Surplus People
Struggle between
Darkness and Oblivion
Conservative Laissez-Faire
"Trickle-Down" Madness

Across America
A Surplus People
Hope each new day
For Freedom's Return
To an America of
Liberty and Justice for All

ONE
JUST SURPLUS

"It really comes down to basic economics. There's no comparative advantage for business in America anymore. The only legitimate goal of our companies is to make money... We can only do that by investing where labor is cheap...taxes are nonexistent and governments are too weak to stop us... We are simply doing what good capitalists...have always done." Derber and Magrass, *The Surplus American*

RULING HIGH TABLE
ANNIVERSARY CONFERENCE
OPENING REMARKS

Chairman: "Ladies and gentlemen. Welcome to our 50th anniversary conference to discuss our national management of the nation's surplus population and this years' critical ongoing events that require our immediate attention.

As you all know, in the 1970s...*the United States went into economic decline, after the costs of the Vietnam War and the rise of Europe and Japan... Clearly, a major source of the trouble in America was that workers, especially educated and unionized workers infected by the 1960s revolts, felt too entitled. They were trying to interfere with our prerogative to run our corporations and to run the world. There was excessive democracy, a democratic distemper that had to be contained.*

We got the American people to agree we had to spend more on armaments as they accept a declining standard of living, while big business profits soar. They identified with us, and our interests became their interest. They...see themselves as part of a great American nation.

And so the Republican Trickle-Down 1981 Revolution opened the world to us by crushing the unions and creating trade agreement...that ensure us global profits. The government subsidized our shift to production abroad... and won the support of the lower classes by making America the Great Superpower again and telling them that money given to us will trickle down to the...more money for us billionaires, lower taxes, fewer regulations...with no conditions.

Actually, the hard truth is that maintaining factories in America had become too expensive. We used the tickle-down free trade and tax policies as incentive to close the remaining American steel mills and America's industrial infrastructure and move production where labor is cheap, where we don't have to worry about environment or occupational health and safe standards.

Of course, in America, with factories closing, inner cities are being abandoned. The jobs that gave blue-collar access to a middle class lifestyle...disappeared. The American dream became an illusion. Rather than wealth trickling down, the Gap between rich and non-rich has grown dramatically. This, my friends, is the legacy of the Republican "Trickle-Down" Revolution. Our Conservative legacy is more prosperity for more billionaires. Surely, the streets of the trickle-down revolution are lined with gold.

That said, *we must address today the fact that we have special problems to consider this year, as the number of parasites and unworthy surplus rabble is increasing* rapidly... *with ten million new unemployed in the last year. This, of course, is consistent with our business strategies over the last four decades...and it demonstrates how profitable our national outsourcing...has been.*

We are seeing even *today the more we can outsource our financial services and dispose of surplus workers, the more profitable our operations have become* ... The problem is *the unworthy elements of the surplus people, the parasite and freeloaders, are questioning the virtues of our national downsizing and outsourcing strategy.* I know you all appreciate *that surplus people are responsible for their own fate. Life is a privilege and they haven't earned it. They* naturally *blame the system rather than themselves for their unemployment and uselessness.* Nevertheless we've known from the beginning that while the surplus population we created *would get Americans to do just about anything...at minimum wages*, in time it would have down the road ramifications. And that time is now before us.

I realize that many don't want to hear that consumer debt is rising along with government debt. But this is very dangerous not just for the US but for the world economy. Deficits are not a problem as long as they stimulate productivity. The trickle-down "supply side" policies of the 1980s created massive deficits *with huge government spending on the military and huge subsidies for* big business that *provided a short-term boom for billionaires.* Our policies, however, have *undermined our long-term competitive advantage by demonizing government, unraveling our industrial infrastructure, and romanticizing the military.*

We must use the government immediately to reinvest in the US and rebuild America itself...and that will require retooling and shifting resources. It may be the wisest policy, but it will also *mean sacrificing the short term for the long term.* It will cost us billionaires. *If we don't…invest billions of government stimulus in America, in jobs for the US surplus population to rebuild our nation, both the US economy and the global economy are doomed. The protesters in the street know this.*

There it is ladies and gentlemen. *I appreciate your being here despite today's protests by the surplus people …This is the biggest domestic disorder so far. We anticipated these protests, but not on a national scale…* We know *our surplus policy marginalizes the masses and doesn't offer them even the illusion that they have any place in our society.* I'm sure most of you agree it is in our best interest that *this must change, and fast…The surplus masses have nothing to lose. All of us here must support a massive shift of our own resources and wealth to fund a social reconstruction of our own country. (pause)*

Now, if we don't wrap up the meeting today, we'll convene again tomorrow until all presentations have been heard. Please enjoy the rest of your evening."

"These capitalists generally act harmoniously and in concert, to fleece the people."

—*Abraham Lincoln*

from his first speech as an Illinois state legislator, 1837

VOICE OF DESPAIR

Suspended in a sea of Corruption,
Poverty, and Despair, I ask myself
"Who Am I" in this Political
Wasteland of Lies and Deceit

Across the Landscape of Freedom,
I see the face of Darkness and Pain
Of Suffering People longing for
Liberty, Truth, and Justice

And in my trepidation, I know
I am nothing, just "Trickle-Down"
Fodder struggling in a Lives for
Profit Predatory Jungle

With each new day I strive to
Survive the Deprivation of
Being "surplus" in a wilderness of
Greed, Corruption, and Injustice

Betrayed, Abandoned, Forgotten
To subsist in Economic Human
Bondage, I live for the return of
Democracy, Freedom, and Truth

TWO

AMERICA BETRAYED

*"Your purpose, then, plainly stated, is
that you will destroy the Government,
unless you be allowed to construe and
enforce the Constitution as you please.
You will rule or ruin in all events."*
Abraham Lincoln
Cooper Union Address, 1860

Sunday Morning

A beautiful morning. The sun is shining; not a cloud in the sky; a soft breeze in the air. A great morning just to be alive. Bill and Martha have just returned home from Sunday church service. As Bill relaxes quietly in his chair, Martha happily goes about preparing their usual Sunday brunch. Martha looks over at Bill, smiles, and says, "Bill, you look as if you have the weight of the world on your shoulders." Bill opens his eyes and smiles at Martha. "Just thinking, my Dear. Did you notice the church was over half empty this morning?" "That's every Sunday, Bill," Martha replies. "I suspect people have come to believe that faith doesn't matter. It's as if God doesn't have a place in their lives anymore."

"It's more than that, Martha," Bill responds. "At its core it's everything that personifies the Conservative "every man for himself" ideological culture of death. Do you realize it's now fifty years since the financial gurus hijacked the Republican party and set about dismantling America's manufacturing prosperity and restructuring America for the sole benefit of the financial power elite? January's Capitol Insurrection to overturn the Constitution and the will of the people is just the culminating event of decades of radical Republican ideological extremism to usurp the people's sovereignty in a final bid for absolute power and the concentration of wealth.

"The Republican Conservative struggle for the Soul of America has been long and unrelenting. What's left, I'm afraid, is the everyday reality that most Americans today struggle to just make it another day. Everything is temporary, Martha, with no thought of the future. I have no doubt that in the fullness of time the "truth" will reveal the extent of the Republican Conservative legislative demise of the American Dream, the middle class, the death of competitive free market capitalism, and the making of America's debt-based financial economy of minimum-wage jobs, desperation and despair. And the Conservative reality for this American moment is ever present in every sphere of America life.

"Today, Martha, concentrated wealth and the Pooring of America are the dominant political-economic features of a decadent America. I often wonder how many of today's voters understand that the 1% own more than the entire middle class, while three billionaires own more than the bottom 50% of America.

"It seems not so long ago, Bill, prosperity shone brightly over an America pleased with itself, healthy and alive," says Martha.

"You're getting old, Martha," replies Bill with a chuckle. But you're right, Martha.

"There was a time not so long ago when the people of America were at economic peace, stable and secure with a strong industrial middle class where everyone had access to a secure productive living-wage job, affordable healthcare, education and housing, and the promise of retirement with dignity in old age.

"All that once seemed to be for a prosperous middle class is now gone, Martha. "All that promise of yesterday's America is no more. "All that was democracy in America that gave life meaning and happiness has been dismantled and discarded to the greed of fairy-tale profits and a financialized casino economy at the expense of an abandoned "surplus" people *"responsible for their own fate."*

"And sadly for our children and grandchildren, all we once cherished that was an America founded on the Sovereignty of the People, the Blessings of Liberty, Representative Democracy and the protection of the "General Welfare" is now but yesterday's promise lost to an impoverished predatory America of individual extremism, greed and corruption."

II

Everyone's talking. But no
One speaks truth to the how
Or why we are a suffering people
Subsisting in human bondage

No one talks of the Republican
Conservative politics of radical
Extremism, absolute power,
And the "survival of the fittest"

> **No one speaks to the tyranny of**
> **The Republican political fanaticism**
> ***"To virtually eliminate the middle Class.***
>
> **No one talks of the Republican**
> **Political carnage and desolation**
> **Of today's America of Want,**
> **Desperation, and Despair**
>
> **No one bears witness to the**
> **Fifty-Year betrayal and plunder of**
> **America's "Profit before People"**
> **Republican "Trickle-Down" politics**

Now, after more than forty years of autocratic Republican legislative governance, the people of America are again asking in the quiet silence of their distress and despair that never ending question: WHY?

WHY is America a nation of excessive income inequality, bankrupt hallowed out communities, decimated families, structural racism, political corruption, and divisive polarization?

WHY is America unable to employ its people with secure living-wage jobs, provide a decent "standard of living," affordable healthcare, education, food, and housing, and a secure dignified retirement?

WHY is more than one out of two Americans living poor struggling to make ends meet in the richest country in the world? WHY does America tolerate sacrificing "Lives" for "Profit" in a democracy founded on "the inalienable right to life"? WHY in the "Promised Land of Democracy, Truth, and Justice do so many who take the oath of office to "support, protect, and defend" the people turn their back on the people? Isn't it time we understand "WHY," why we are an abandoned "surplus" people struggling to exist in an America of concentrated wealth and despair in the richest country in the world?

To comprehend the political, cultural, and economic realities of this American moment is to understand that the "truth" lies buried, all but hidden from the *"inattention of the people to the concerns of their government,"* concealed by the deception and deceit of lies, false promises, and alternate facts. America's presidents for decades have cautioned the nation to "face the truth." President Jimmy Carter in his 1979 presidential address, *"Crisis of Confidence,"* warned America that today's government *"designed for the people"* has *"gotten into the hands...of special interests...an invisible empire...set up above the forms of democracy."* The Founding Fathers cautioned against the rise of concentrated economic power that takes away liberty. Abraham Lincoln warned of the greed and corruption of *the "money powers."* And Republican President Theodore Roosevelt defiantly spoke of the *"invisible government owing no allegiance...to the people"* that sits enthroned *"behind the ostensible government."*

History's warning is today's American reality. In sharp contrast to America's Declaration of Independence and Constitutional guarantees enacted to protect the "General Welfare," the Republican Conservative "big money" power ideological agenda of the last five decades has achieved the political economy of *"every man for himself"* individual extremism: *the "freedom from of obligations; freedom from responsibility; freedom to fend for oneself"* *and the freedom to starve."*

Today we all experience in one way or another the Republican subsistence debt-based America of poverty wages and an unaffordable standard of living. The Republican freedom of "individual extremism" is today the people's political-economic reality of the Conservative political license to steal and destroy in the name of profit. The Republican "Pooring of America" fulfills Daniel Webster's warning – that *"our overthrow...should it come ...will be...from the inattention of the people to the concerns of their government…falling prey to the dupes of designing men and become the instruments of their own undoing".*

And come they did in the seventies with a vengeance. They came with the ruthlessness of the "designing men" of 1873, 1893, 1907, and 1929. And in the Nineteen Eighties the economic power brokers hyped the Republican "Trickle-Down" Revolution, dismantled America's industrial economy, transformed the people's manufacturing industrial base into a deregulated rogue economy of casino capitalism, and laid the groundwork for the deconstruction of America's democratic institutions.

This is simply the reality of the power of America's financial plutocracy, an American oligarchic monolithic system of political economic dominance over American democracy that is at the heart of America's concentration of wealth in the top 1%, the "Pooring of America," and, another coming financial collapse. The continual rise of today's inflationary surge of rising prices on everything across America irrespective of the needs of society is simply "laissez-faire" redistribution of the people's limited resources through price gouging that demonstrates America's deregulated "free" market economic system of supply and demand is dead.

Should doubt remain, forget we not, the Republican lies, disinformation, and deceit that seek autocratic power supremacy lingers in our midst to hold captive the reality of truth that perpetuates today's inequality and injustice in every aspect of American life.

III

When No One Feels
The Pain,
The Desperation,

And Despair,
Of a suffering People
Exploited, Abandoned
And Forgotten,
The Flame of Liberty
Shines brightly for
The OPPRESSED
Longing for an inclusive
Democracy of Freedom
And Justice for All

Enter James McGill Buchanan, the Nineteen Sixties political-economic "intellectual of the embattled Jim Crow South" and pioneer of the Conservative decades' Republican assault on America's democracy. In time Buchanan's political theories would disempower the electoral majority and shift people power to America's kleptocratic ruling elite. Buchanan believed that the people must be prevented from using the public power of representative democracy if the "supremacy of capital" was to survive. He saw an American world dominated by the wealthiest and most powerful. His goal was a private governing class of the financial power elite freed from public accountability. Buchanan's strategy became a secretive political agenda to revise the political dynamics of democratic governance.

Catherine MacLean, in *Democracy in Chains: The Deep History of the Radical Right's Stealth Plan for America*, describes the strategy Buchanan and his collaborators "developed to disempower the political majority." The Buchanan stealth strategy, backed by unlimited "dark money," called for a *"stealth takeover of the Republican Party as its delivery mechanism,"* and a stealth agenda to "kill off" the unions, limit voting rights, privatize everything from public resources to Social Security and Medicare, reframe the tax laws to limit wealthy taxation and direct taxation to the little people, deregulate the rule of law, deny climate change, and transform the legal system into *"a new jurisprudence…to make the protection and enhancement of corporate profits and private wealth the cornerstone of the legal system."*

The Republican political establishment, politically backed by unlimited "dark money," in 1980 implemented Buchanan's political-economic theory of capital supremacy and the Powell strategic stealth plan for the Conservative takeover of America. The Republican plan designed to "save capitalism from democracy," focused on placing legal restraints on public officials to prevent them "from using public power," take down democracy with a cadre of "true believers" for whom compromise is a dirty word," purge the party of "old time" Republicans, and "force elected officials" in every red state to do the party's bidding or "lose their seats." Today the Republican Party of "old" is no more.

In 1971, the Republican party elite came armed with the "Powell Memorandum," the strategic blueprint written by Lewis Powell to the U.S. Chamber of Commerce to save the *"free enterprise system" from democracy."* The plan outlined the method and means to undermine America's democratic institutions, restructure the American economy to unhampered capital supremacy, and financially vandalize an economically secure democratic people. Then in 1980, the new "hijacked" Republican political establishment embarked on a political propaganda campaign of lies and deceit promising "Trickle-Down" prosperity for "everyone, including the poor," in a skillfully scripted crusade shrouded in political smoke and mirrors.

The Republican political Conservative ideological triumph of 1980 established the Republican political establishment as the delivery mechanism for the Conservative "big money" subjugation and political takeover of American democracy. The drive to de-industrialize the people's economic prosperity to "financialize" the American economy, and eliminate the "middle class" majority set in motion the Conservative strategic blueprint to remake America into a kleptocracy of wealth, power, and privilege.

The American economic apocalypse of this American moment is the reality of those "designing men," of the Nineteen Seventies, as Richard Clarke reminds us, *to virtually eliminate the middle class majority in America.*" It is the political-economic reality of the Conservative "political economy" promulgated by James BUCHANAN to disempower America's electoral majority from using the public power of representative democracy to survive in an American "Trickle-Down" world dominated by the wealthiest and most powerful freed from public accountability: Milton FREIDMAN, champion of deregulated "laissez-faire" markets and maximization of shareholder value as the sole purpose and social responsibility of capitalism; Robert BORK, advocate of operational efficiencies over competition through mergers and acquisitions; and Lewis POWELL, author of the Conservative 1971 grand strategic blueprint to *save capitalism from democracy,*" and the Conservative 1981 Republican "Trickle-Down Supply Side" Revolution that 'promised universal prosperity for all' but delivered the people of America an engineered financialized subsistence debt-based casino economy of want, desperation, and despair.

The new Republican political-economic reality, today controlled by anti-democratic "maga" extremists, is the new Republican political order of "designing men" tasked to suppress democracy through the manipulative control of state power, and overthrow the ability of representative government to protect the "General Welfare" and the human and civil rights of a Constitutional America.

After decades of "Trickle-Down" financial greed and political corruption, this may will be America's world of tomorrow should "We the People" allow a Republican "voter suppression" seizure of power succeed in 2024. The human tragedy of the Conservative extremism of the *"survival of the fittest"* is at the threshold of becoming the forever Republican political economic reality of oppression that will hold America hostage in an impoverished web of tyrannical greed and corruption.

IV

"The Private sector Thrives Best with Minimal State involvement …" GOVERNMENT'S ROLE in the Conservative "trickle-down" state is limited to "CONTROL the surplus population;" ADVANCE state policies that "eliminate" government regulation, and wealthy and corporate taxation; PROVIDE for "off-shore" jobs incentives, subsidies, trade policies that send jobs abroad;" and SUPPORT government disinvestment of America's infrastructure by describing the infrastructure itself and as socialism."
Derber & Magrass, *The Surplus American*

As the "designing men" of wealth, power, and greed proceeded to pillage and plunder America, dismantle the institutions of Constitutional democracy, curb the rights of the people, ravage America's prosperous communities, they destroyed America's ability to employ its people with secure living-wage employment.

The domestic financial "colonization" of America is the political and economic reality of the takeover, subjugation, and "Pooring of America." The Republican political establishment, bearer of the sword of Darwinian imperialism and the ideology of the *"survival of the fittest"* individual extremism, ruthlessly descended on the people of America in 1981 in the pursuit of absolute power and capital supremacy over American democracy.

In one historic electoral moment based on promises of false prosperity and national greatness, the Republican "Trickle-Down" Revolution, in the absence of any public scrutiny, gave rise to a new ruling power elite. The Conservative ideological political agenda of radical extremism gave way to a *"survival of the fittest"* political mandate to disenfranchise the American people, deconstruct American democracy, and financialize America. And in less than a decade the Republican political establishment accomplished history's greatest mass exploitation of a free democratic people.

The Republican "Trickle Down" Revolution that would come to revolutionize America's political and economic way of life, impoverish the American people, and institutionalize the unhampered supremacy of capital is the story of the financial takeover of America. It is also a chronicle of political-economic greed, political corruption, lies and deceit, and the power of "dark money" and "designing men" documented by Donald Bartlett and James Steels in *The Betrayal of the American Dream*; William Greider, *Who Will Tell the People*; Jane Mayer, *Dark Money*; Hedrick Smith, *Who Stole the American Dream*), and Thom Hartmann, *Screwed: The Undeclared War Against the Middle Class*. Tragically for today's America, few among us were listening, and fewer Americans to this day understand little of today's crushing reality of the Republican Fifty-Year unraveling of American democracy to the supremacy of capital and Conservative political-economic dominance over America.

V

**We've heard the empty
Promises of "designing men"**

**We've borne the trauma of
Want, desperation, and despair**

**We've endured the treachery of
Disloyalty, betrayal, and sedition**

Lewis Powell saw the success of organized labor and the cry for human and civil liberties as a middle class *"assault on the free enterprise system"* and the cause for the decline in America's industrial profitability. His subsequent political manifesto formulated the Conservative ideological political strategy for the Republican political establishment to politically subvert American democracy, undermine the democratic political process, and subjugate the people of America to the disenfranchisement of a new politically created predatory "Trickle-Down" subsistence economy of concentrated wealth.

The Powell strategic blueprint for Republican political domination and concentration of wealth in the hands of a few triggered the mobilization of America's "big money" vested interests to embark on a quiet - low-key - long-term - well-funded political campaign to secure the transformation of American governance to *"save capitalism from democracy."*

The Republican political betrayal of America by the Conservative political establishment for a social-economic transformation of America and political-economic dominance over American democracy set in motion the Republican Conservative Supremacy Agenda.

FIRST they moved to **REVOKE the "rule of law" and oversight accountability** through the **DEREGULATION** of finance, business, politics, and the media; and then *PROCEEDED* with relentless, remorseless, and ruthless resolve to:

ABOLISH wealthy and corporate taxation through periodic Republican trillion dollar tax cuts, tax rate deductions, tax exemptions and loopholes;

BUILD a Conservative predatory "Trickle-Down" economy of *"every man for himself"* ideological "individual extremism" of the *"survival of the fittest"* in a Profit over People" concentration of wealth financial America;

CREATE a "white supremacist" majority in pursuit of a white nationalist Conservative agenda of ideological extremism and political dominance;

DECONSTRUCT the machinery of government and America's democratic institutions;

DISMANTLE America's community-centered industrial infrastructure and with it America's ability to employ an abandoned "surplus" people *"left to their own fate";*

DISCREDIT free press journalism to shield and defend the Republican political "Trickle-Down" core agenda of political lies and disinformation, false narratives, and conspiracy theories to politically disrupt, divide, and polarize the American people;

ELIMINATE Social Security, Medicare, and Medicaid and the Social Safety Net through massive periodic and disguised budget cuts;

LAY the foundation for the political takeover of American democracy.

LIMIT voter access to the ballot through voter electoral suppression laws and voter certification barriers;

OBSTRUCT democratic populist policies and legislation that support the "common good" and the "general fare" of the people;

PRIVATIZE public services, public lands, and America's natural resources to private sector contractors of "big money" political financial support;

POLITICIZE the judiciary to enshrine private wealth, protect the laissez-faire economy of "Profit over People," block congressional oversight accountability, water-down government regulation, and stifle reform;

REMOLD America's political, judicial, and academic state of mind to the Conservative mindset of "Trickle-Down" individual extremism;

SECURE political "dark money" dominance over state legislatures.

The success of the "big money" power elite of "designing men" in the political-economic takeover of yesterday's American Conservatism is today's Republican legislated Profit over People "Trickle-Down" state. And the hijacked Republican political establishment for every working American today is the Conservative *"survival of the fittest"* America of *"every man for himself"* individual extremism.

Today we struggle as a People of Liberty in an America dominated by an entrenched Conservative ideological Social Darwinism that is the Republican supremacy of capital and a democracy of want, desperation, and despair. The Republican four decades of politically engineered pillage and plunder of the American people has destroyed America's industrial prosperity, cultural values, and the well-being and security of the American family. The Republican political victory of radical Conservative extremism in one unguarded electoral moment is tragically the Conservative "maga" political-economic reality of this American moment.

VI

**How sweet the sound of Liberty
It soothes our sorrows, heals our
Wounds, and drives away our fears**

**Our strength is in the things we
Value: Truth, Equality, Justice,
Family, Dignity, and Respect**

**The time is now we assert who
We are: either we are a People of
Liberty ... OR WE ARE NOTHING!**

Overnight the Republican political establishment of 1980, gave birth to a Conservative "Trickle-Down" *"you're on your own"* political platform that shamelessly asserted American capitalism didn't *"need America any more…Surplus people are responsible for their own fate."* America ceased to be a nation of the freedoms fought and won in the blood of our Sons and Fathers, the *"Freedom from Want, Freedom from Hunger, and the Freedom from Fear."* These are the freedoms upon which President Franklin Roosevelt declared that *"Liberty requires an opportunity to make a living which gives not only enough to live by, but something to live for"* that today have all but become entombed in an American graveyard of imperial greed and corruption.

The tragic reality is the "designing men" of wealth and power in our time have ruthlessly destroyed America's competitive "free market economy" of supply and demand. The economics of national prosperity for the many has been transformed into a laissez-faire "Trickle-Down" subsistence debt-based casino economy of monopoly power supremacy. America's democracy of the people has been politically transformed in every sector of American life into a "deregulated" state of debt liability, taxation for the little people, and unavoidable poverty engendered by the power of concentrated wealth.

Our national inattention to the concerns of our government has led to the functional undoing of every governing institution, including the Supreme Court and the legislative branch, where precedent parliamentary procedure established over the centuries has been "politically" corrupted and manipulated to the Conservative political agenda. Every Republican act and word spoken is couched in the deceit and deception of the political interests of the "big money" power elite that consider the people *"economically illiterate, culturally backward, and demographically irrelevant."*

We see at every level of the Republican political establishment, ruthless "designing men" of wealth and power that seek to undermine the people's democratic process and seize absolute authoritarian power. These are the "designing men" that Vice President Henry Wallace warned America to beware: the money changers, the profiteers, the usurpers *"who claim to be super patriots…but would destroy every liberty guaranteed by the Constitution; demand free enterprise, but…are spokesmen for monopoly and vested interests; their final objective…to capture political power [to] keep the common man in eternal subjugation."*

The Conservative politics of political dominance, individual extremism, and economic subjugation "overshadows" all that America values in this 2024 electoral moment. For a democratic republic "of the people" committed to "Liberty and Justice for all," today's Conservative radical extremism of lies, disinformation, and deceit, racial polarization, white supremacy politics, and voter suppression is the "fascist" road to autocracy. The America of 2024 beckons every citizen of democracy to take an affirmative stand to restore America to a nation of Freedom, Equality, and Justice.

TYRANNY OF GREED

TODAY AMERICA
"We the People"
Are
A PEOPLE DECEIVED
BY REPUBLICAN GREED
"Big Money" Tyranny
And
Concentrated Wealth

TODAY AMERICA
"We the People"
Are
A PEOPLE DESPERATE
Through the
REPUBLICAN CORRUPTION
of
Vulture Capitalism

TODAY AMERICA
"We the People"
Are
A PEOPLE SUFFERING
From
REPUBLICAN DEREGULATION
and
Capital Supremacy

THREE
RULED BY THIEVES

> The "money powers prey upon the nation
> in times of peace and conspire against it in
> times of adversity," then brazenly denounce
> as "enemies all who question its methods or
> throw light upon its crimes."
> **President Abraham Lincoln**

The new Republican political-economic reality is today controlled by anti-democratic "maga" extremists dedicated to suppress democracy through the manipulative control of state power, and the overthrow of the ability of representative government to protect the "General Welfare" and the human rights of a Constitutional people. We are, as Jim Hightower writes in *Thieves in High Places, "a people ruled by thieves"* controlled *"by a ruling class of moneyed elites that usurps liberty…transferring money and power from the many… to the few."*

Welcome to the Conservative *"survival of the fittest"* predatory world of "surplus" people *"responsible for their own fate."* This is today's forty-year Republican political-economic triumph over a once prosperous people transformed into a "surplus" left behind struggling to survive the Conservative "Trickle-Down" empire of capital supremacy, wage poverty, and racial injustice.

In today's Republican world of "Lives for Profit" radical individual extremism, the ideology of the *"survival of the fittest"* offers "freedom" without responsibility to a privileged power elite. For the rest of America, the Republican ideological imperative of "individual extremism" means the "freedom" to fend for oneself and support a family on subsistence wages in the absence of affordable healthcare, and the means to survive in any meaningful way.

The Republican subsistence "Trickle-Down society that promised "prosperity for everyone" in 1981 is the "Trickle-Down" political-economic reality that destroyed American capitalism of free competition, gutted America's industrial prosperity, and financialized the American economy into a political-economic engine of wealth concentration for the top 1%. And characteristic of the lies and deceit of greed and corruption of the Republican "Trickle-Down" miracle of wealth creation, there followed financial scandals of corporate fraud, insider trading, foreclosure abuse, stock manipulation, financial growth gimmicks, hedge fund profiteers, and the "soft money" plunder of America's worker pension funds. And, naturally, the profiteers say this is the just the "invisible hand" of fluctuating markets that just happened to give way to America's 2008 financial collapse and, of course, the taxpayer trillion-dollar "speculation" bailouts that continue to this day to add trillion-dollar debt to America's "Trickle-Down" casino economy.

Between 1981 and 2000, America's productivity increased by some 70% while wages remained all but stagnant. And the earnings of the top 1% and 0.1% increased 158% and 341% respectively. For the "surplus" left behind, however, *Time* (August 2/9, 2021) reports that since 1979 the cumulative change in real hourly wages for American workers rose but 3% for the bottom 10 percent and 15% for the middle third of the workforce. Tragically, the record also shows that the top 1% own America while over half of America's workers subsist on a low-wage income *"making an average wage of $10.22 an hour."*

Look around the neighborhood, open up the newspaper, turn on the evening news, and we see a people of democracy polarized and divided by the radicalized extremism of truth denied, racial xenophobia, political violence, and the inability of the average American to sustain the basic needs of American life.

We share as a People of Liberty a "Land of the Free" unrecognizable from a generation ago, an impoverished *"survival of the fittest"* America of at least 180 million Americans living poor or on the edge of poverty; two out of three working Americans existing on a subsistence wage while over 40 million Americans, including 13 million children, go to bed hungry. We see a Republican politically engineered society of "surplus" people desperately trapped in a ruthless quagmire of institutional decay struggling in silent desperation for the sole benefit of the financial power elite.

Everywhere we look we see the suffering and pain and ever present carnage and desperation of the Fifty-Year Republican "Pooring of America," from the tens of thousands of rusting factories to the latest shut down of America's remaining automotive manufacturing plants. We feel the distress and misery of an abandoned "surplus" people politically condemned to the "Trickle-Down collateral damage of the Republican financialized "freedom to choose" culture of death: a Conservative ideological universe of unrelenting political decadence. We see a democratic people politically ravaged economically and morally condemned to subsist in bankrupt impoverished communities all across America. We see a free democratic people victimized from the annual trauma of over 100,000 "opioid" deaths, 90,000 suicides; 40,000 violent gun deaths, including some 600 massacres, and over 1,000 enforcement fatalities.

This is today's everyday reality of the Republican "Trickle-Down" America of the *"survival of the fittest."* The Republican ownership of death and suffering is the America of "anything goes" in the pursuit of Profit and Power at any cost: an unregulated

"Big Pharma" multi-billion dollar "opioid" profit scheme that has killed over a million Americans; a burning planet fueled by fossil energy profits; and a Republican violent "insurrection" to overturn the will of the people to maintain political power.

II

***"America's megabanks and policy
makers are continuing a program …
the ultimate result of which will be
to virtually eliminate the middle class
majority in America."***
Richard Clark
"Why is America Suffering?"

Yesterday's American prosperity is today an America of consolidated wealth, the demise of wealthy and corporate taxation, capital supremacy, and for everybody else, an America of *"every man for himself'"* In 1981, Republican legislation reduced wealthy taxation from a 70% high to today's 7.2% for millionaires and 3.2% for the top one tenth of America's taxpayers. Eighty-three percent of the Republican trillion "tax cut" of 2017 went to the top 1% and reduced the corporate tax rate from 35% to 21%. In 2020, the wealth of the richest 1% of Americans increased by over $7 trillion while the 55 most profitable companies in America paid "zero" taxes, and the 400 wealthiest households paid an overall tax rate less than any income group in America. How is it in America any individual can hold a $500 million a year position and pay virtually no taxes? Well, it's not difficult to understand when we realize, as one of America's most privileged aristocratic elite famously remarked, *"Only the little people pay taxes!"*

This is the Republican 1981 promise that "Trickle- Down economics" would make everyone prosper. This is today's America of the *"survival of the fittest"* Republican upward redistribution of income to the top 1%. Given the historical reality of feudal societies of concentrated wealth, caste privilege, and disposable people, it follows that the Republican "Trickle-Down" society of concentrated wealth and aristocratic privilege is a class stratified world of wealth and power.

America in 2023 has *"the widest wealth gap between the rich and the poor of any industrial country."* We see America's billionaires today worth more than double the cumulative wealth of the bottom 156 million poorest Americans. According to Professor Davis Markovits of the Yale Law School as reported in *Time* (May 10/17, 2021), *"the richest 5% of American households own two-thirds of the country's total wealth... The economic inequality that separates the rich from the rest of us has become so great ...[that] to reduce inequality and honor shared citizenship is to tax wealth... World history teaches that oligarchies are almost impossible to unwind... Extreme wealth inequality confronts the U.S. with a civilizational threat. Wealth taxes answer the threat."* Here we see taxation is the unmistakable Conservative reality of absolute legislative power of vested donor based inequality that has impoverished American people without political constraint or accountability.

It is in this context, the Republican Conservative ideological *"survival of the fittest"* "Lives for Profit" culture is akin to the "fascist" ideological imperative that *"human beings,"* as Samuel Goldman points out, *"are raw material to be used or disposed of... in a disenchanted world of slavery and terror."*

The Conservative "core values" that drive the Republican "Culture of Death" in America hold in common the Social Darwin political-economic theory of the *"survival of the fittest,"* the *"superiority" of a ruling elite, and every human being is "responsible for his own fate."* Similarly, The Republican "Trickle-Down" political-economic Conservatism of radical extremism champions the idea of power supremacy and justification for the creation of wealth at whatever the cost to human life, the community, and the environment. Everything on the planet is a commodity subject to the taking of the power brokers in the pursuit of profit and wealth."

Conservative radical extremism stresses *"the dominant group that secures and holds power"* is the *"best fit"* to exercise power." Historian Bruce Ingalls in *The Opium War*, points out that the 19th Century economic theory of political economy of Malthus, Ricardo, and McCulloch advocated the worker has *"no right to more than a bare living for themselves and their families…if they earned more, it could be taken from them by the landowners in the form of rent, or the state in the form of…taxes."* [That the] *"alternative for many families might be starvation"*? [Well], *"this form of culling was necessary…to prevent overpopulation."*

The Conservative extremism of *"power dominance"* and *the "survival of the fittest"* rationalized by the American political economists Buchanan, Friedman, and Bork to justify the "Pooring of America" is today the "dark money" funded "Trickle-Down" America of political economy, wealth concentration, and monopoly dominance. The Republican 1981 "Trickle-Down" Revolution of "political economy" has accomplished the "big money" Conservative power agenda of political-economic dominance over the welfare and security of America. we are as a "surplus" people the "collateral damage" persevering in want, desperation, and despair in an everyday struggle to survive subsistence wages, a rising already unaffordable Cost of Living; a staggering national debt of some 30 trillion dollars; 140 billion dollars in unpaid medical debt; over 1.7 trillion dollars in "forever" student loan debt; and 13 trillion dollars in credit card debt.

The sad reality here of want and despair, the French historian Georges Lefebvre in *The Coming of the French Revolution*, records a fitting lament of a French patriot in a similar time, *"I look with compassion upon the cruel tempest with which my country is threatened, shed tears to see so many…reduced to such a profound misery."*

III

**I see far and near the "Senseless
Misery" of "Trickle-Down" corruption,
Political betrayal, and racial injustice**

**I bear the pain of a disenfranchised
Surplus people politically deceived,
Abandoned, and forgotten**

**I behold the torment of hopelessness,
A desperate mother's despair, the
Chains of the mass incarcerated**

**I share the quiet grief of a
Suffering people longing for
Liberty and Justice for All**

Since the dawn of the Republican "Trickle-Down" Revolution of 1981, four decades of Republican political dominance have reduced over half the population of America to a state of want, desperation, and despair. This is the political-economic condition of America that came with the rise of unhampered capital supremacy, the Pooring of America, and the death of American people's industrial economic lifeline. With the loss of secure living wage jobs in every mill town across America, the security and stability of America's prosperous middle class disappeared, and the people of America became just discarded "surplus" labor in a subsistence debt-based casino economy *responsible for their own fate.*

The heart of the Republican "Trickle-Down" Revolution was the deindustrialization of America's manufacturing economy and the outsourcing of American labor to off-shore cheap foreign labor and big profits. The privatization of public services, the creation of a Republican legislated money-driven economy of financial instruments and debt-based poverty followed.

In the Nineteen Sixties, before the rise of the Conservative revolution of the "survival of the fittest" subsistence *"every man for himself"* economy, the United States produced 96% of what it consumed. Hundreds of thousands of mill towns and factory cities across America supported an economic miracle the envy of the world. America's children graduated from high school to work in local industries secure in a lifetime of stable family living-wage jobs, affordable family healthcare, and the promise of a dignified retirement. Downtown America prospered and life was good in an American world that offered a strong standard of living that provided a family home, family vacation, and the promise of opportunity for the next generation.

All that disappeared with the advent of the 1971 Republican Powell strategy to "save" American capitalism from democracy. And the 1981 Republican "Trickle-Down" Revolution that followed transformed America into a "laissez-faire" financialized casino economy of fairy-tale short-term profits, subsistence wage labor, and wealth concentration.

With the elimination of America's manufacturing prosperity, hundreds of thousands of mill towns and factory cities across America lost their livelihood and reason for existence. Tens of millions of jobs forever lost, whole industries wiped out, and America's working class deprived of meaningful work. All that remained were hollowed out towns of once prosperous small businesses, and the rise of monopoly owned box-stores, strip malls of fast-food franchises and discount stores, and widespread poverty. America became a parking lot in the struggle for bankrupt communities to survive the shock, horror, and desperation of instant poverty with no available means of survival.

An abandoned factory town is not just a plant closing. It's a street scene from the apocalypse, the removal of all that gives life, meaning, and purpose to the community. Without work, the life-blood of the community evaporates. People are left isolated, helpless, and desperate; marriages and families fall apart while civil institutions and community church life slowly die. As the economic deprivation of the community intensifies, the social fabric and connectedness of the community disintegrates along with a devaluation of life itself that inevitability gives rise to the moral breakdown of society to addiction and violence, the marginalization of the poor, xenophobic hate mongering, and political polarization. This is the story of America's once prosperous communities and the descent of the people of America into "Trickle-Down" poverty in an America that now produces less than 4% percent of what it consume.

The loss of America's industrial economic prosperity in the drive to create a subsistence-wage, debt-based casino economy, as Chris Hedges writes in *American Fascists*, "*turned…most towns… into a wilderness of poverty and urban decay…Despair is the common denominator that shares a common feeling of loss, of abandonment, and deep pessimism about the future. When despair is this profound the desperate begin to seek miracles. It is easier, indeed understandable, to look for hope and comfort in the mystical hand.*"

As long as America's communities struggle to subsist in economic desperation, and the people of America remain demoralized and hungry in a financialized economy committed to wealth creation for a few, life for the many living in "quiet desperation" will remain polarized without purpose or meaning. The profiteers will continue to hunt down the poor; the hopes and cries of the helpless will gradually fade and die; and the darkness of evil will forever enslave a suffering People to the greed and corruption of the Conservative "trickle-down" world that destroys all who seek to be free.

The history of greed and power reminds us that a nation that denies its citizens the ability to earn a decent living from productive living-wage work is a nation bankrupt in moral and economic free fall. Is the reign of unhindered capital supremacy over a

Republican politically engineered "surplus" people responsible for their own fate to be the Conservative *"survival of the fittest"* America of the 21ˢᵗ Century? Are we to become an institutionalized "surplus" People of Liberty forever struggling to "make ends meet" in subsistence-wage serfdom?

Alexander Solzhenitzyn is said to have remarked that free people that take for granted their democracy would never surrender to totalitarianism. Unfortunately for America, the tyranny of greed did come to America in 1981, with the Republican seizure of power and the Republican "Trickle-Down" Revolution.

And, then, in 2016, there sat in the shadows of inequity an authoritarian demagogue on a "white horse" ready to promise "better times" to an abandoned "surplus" people - poor, desperate, and alone. That promise of better times, of course, like the Republican 1981 promise of "prosperity for all," would instead bring to America the meaning of "authoritarianism" and the making of "dictatorship" through violent "insurrection." This is the Conservative political reality that seeks to destroy American democracy through the corruption, lies, and disinformation of "designing Men." In the words of Abraham Lincoln, "designing men" who would *destroy the government unless they be allowed to construe and enforce the Constitution as they please.*"

I am reminded that Benjamin Franklin on hearing the comment, *"We have a Republic,"* is said to have rejoined, *"If we can keep it."* I would think if Jean-Jacques Rousseau had been in the room he would have heartedly quipped, "of course, Franklin," *"we may acquire liberty, but it is never recovered if it is lost."* This is the terrifying and sober reality of American democracy today and our future as a People of Liberty.

IV

A republic founded on
Freedom, Truth, and Justice

**turned upside into want,
Desperation and Despair
is a nation dying in the
greed and corruption
of designing men.**

Rousseau was given to observe long before "the worst of times" of 1789, that *"democracy is not compatible with an excessive inequality of wealth."*

In *The Coming of the French Revolution*, French historian Georges Lefebvre points out that the Revolution of 1789 was *"above all the conquest of equal rights."* The aristocrats of France in 1789 were the" tax exempt" predatory brokers of wealth, power and privilege of the country. They held absolute political-economic dominance over the land and the people. The ordinary people labored in a daily struggle to survive on a subsistence income obligated to bread, taxes, and rents. The demands of the people for systemic change in 1789 were *"the issues that caused the conflict to break out"* - individual liberty, equal taxation, equality before the law, and political reform. The people of the land who bore the burden of taxation in needless poverty believed they should *"be able to live on their work;"* the standard of living should *"be proportionate to their wages;"* and government that gives a "free hand" to business and the aristocracy, should *"take measures to assure the right of everyone to a living."*

Invoking the "rights of man", the people laid the foundation of the "Declaration of the Rights of Man and the Citizen" of 1789, which simply affirmed ***"LIBERTY CONSISTS IN THE ABILITY TO DO WHATEVER DOES NOT HARM ANOTHER."***

Now in our desperate moment of subsistence-wage deprivation, desperation, and despair, we are a people given to feel the reality of "Grim Reaper" authoritarian politics of "big money" "political extremism," excessive inequality of wealth, and the demise of

America's "working" middle class majority. With the Republican fiscal policies of the last forty years directed to massive wealthy tax cuts and annual record budget deficits, and subsistence-wage labor, there is an evident parallel world between the predatory "Trickle-Down" Conservative fiscal dominance over America today and the privileged French aristocracy of 1789. The politics and privileges of both are but the same with the same consequences.

The average American worker is unable to make a decent living. Absent national political-economic reforms aimed at a livable-wage and a national fair and equitable tax policy, the Republican "feudal" tax policies of today, as with the French government of 1789, cannot *"raise by direct taxes revenue at all proportionate to the real wealth of the country, or to its legitimate needs."* That the French Revolution was necessary, Yale historian R.R. Palmer concludes, *"the old government simply failed to function, and its officials either would not or could not take the necessary measures necessary to maintain political life."*

As with the 1789 French political nightmare of aristocratic greed and entitlement, the Republican subsistence "Trickle-Down" political-economy has failed the American people in favor of the financial power elite.. The working people of America subsist on pittance wages while a once prosperous America is at any given moment on the verge of economic collapse. And today the ashes of the Conservative ideological quagmire of Republican lies, scheming, and corruption nullify any hope for a better America any time soon.

After decades of Republican abandonment and destruction of America's communities, jobs, and way of life, the people's day of reckoning showed itself in November 2020, as the people of America came together in desperation to cry out as did David long ago in a moment of national peril, greed, and corruption remarked: *"The greedy hunt the poor... They mock their enemies... They delight in telling lies... All have become corrupt."*

The challenges before us are dauntingly real. With a renewed sense of community, we can, and will, redress as a People of Democracy the painful Republican political abandonment of America, and return the land of Washington, Jefferson, and Lincoln to a nation of Freedom and Justice committed to the "General Welfare" and the "Blessings of Liberty."

JUST SURPLUS

People gather
People destitute
People alone

One asks another
Do I know you
The stranger answers

Like you Brother
A pitiful Unworthy
A wretched Nobody

Today just Surplus
Discarded and Forgotten
Lost in the Silence

You are a sovereign being with the unalienable right to live freely, without the threat of intimidation or force from other individuals and oppressive institutions.

FOUR
POLITICAL DELUSION

Louis Brandeis
Supreme Court Justice
*"The people of the United States are
now confronted with an emergency
more serious than war."*

Monday, November 3, 2025

The Med-B-Crisis is spreading out of control while indifferent politicians of the "survival of the fittest" administration refuse to respond with any collective action: "People have to understand that healthcare is not a matter of state policy; healthcare is everyone's individual responsibility." As Bob and Liz of the city's Crisis Response Unit engage in small talk, Liz looks up at Bob, "Something's on your mind."

Bob smiles, "Nothing I can do anything about." "That sounds ominous," Liz says. "Well, it's like this, Liz." "Last year the Republicans seized power through nationwide voter rights suppression laws, voter district gerrymandering, and a "big money" radical right-wing campaign of lies, disinformation, and division. Less than half of the American electorate went to the polls and the "permissible" minority vote was the lowest in decades. Now, in less than a year, the Republicans have consolidated their "authoritarian" dominance with the election of a political demagogue, raised taxes to pay for the new wealthy trillion dollar tax cuts, discontinued all family assistance programs, abandoned infrastructure renewal, climate control, and healthcare assistance, and capped the minimum wage."

Suddenly, a red alert call comes in for 13 Grace Avenue. Arriving at the scene they find a young woman lying unconscious on the pavement. Liz looks up at Bob: "Looks like RDX." Bob asks, "What's her Citizen Validation Quotient"? "Just a minute, "Liz says. "Ok, here we are, her CVQ reads: 'Marilyn Jones, Category 3 Sustainer, 32, divorced, two children, service worker, no life-sustaining healthcare coverage." Bob, now resigned to the Conservative Individual Healthcare Protocol, says, "She'll have to go to the SEC (Surplus Euthanasia Center)." Liz, feeling numb, angrily responds, "We're taking this woman to the Hospital!"

Visibly shaken, Bob walks slowly toward the emergency vehicle thinking to himself: 'NOW CALM DOWN! This is the reality of the new Republican "individual responsibility" healthcare system of "Creators, Producers, Sustainers, Freeloaders, and Parasites..."

"BUT THEN...when this crisis is over, LOOK OUT, over 30 million American workers will have permanently lost their jobs, the Hedge Fund and Private Equity raiders will race to clean out what remains of America's profitable small business ownership, the Investment Banks will fraudulently foreclose on millions of home mortgages, and the "predatory lenders" and "rent collectors" will come to life to scoop up the last dime and few possessions of the evicted and down and out. And what little remained of yesterday's America will be no more... Not really surprising, I guess... The Roman Empire ceased to expand when there was finally no one left to plunder,

and the vultures turned inward to rob the masses and the state until the system just collapsed under the weight of corruption, duplicity, and betrayal. Well, here we go again.'

II

Now as we consider the possibilities of a new age of Freedom, Equality, and Justice, the electoral possibilities of 2024 offer the people of America a return to the values and beliefs of the Founding Fathers - that is, insofar as the majority of the electorate are willing to *"accept [the] responsibility"* to exercise *"the right, the power, and the duty to protect [our] own welfare."*

The Constitution of these United States is the "living" promise of the people's rights that work only to the extent "We the People" are willing to support, protect, and defend that promise against all enemies both "foreign and domestic." By "domestic" is to say the shadow of "designing men" of wealth, power, and privilege that seek to hold political dominance over today's body politic and the wealth of America. It is here that history's most sober and cautionary saga reminds us that only a politically free sovereign people in control of their own political destiny can and will provide for the future freedom and prosperity of generations to come.

In the richest country in the world there is enough for every American to enjoy a productive, healthy, and peaceful life. In a representative democracy committed to a constitutional order that protects, promotes, protects, and defends the "public welfare," the people are assured a share of the "blessings of liberty. Certainly it's not an attack on freedom as the proponents of "individual extremism" claim: IT IS FREEDOM! It is as President Theodore Roosevelt affirmed in an earlier desperate time: *"The only prosperity worth having"* is that which affects the mass of the people... It is our duty to see that the wage worker, the* *small producer, the ordinary consumer…get their fair share of the benefit of business prosperity".*

"The most perfect political community" declared Aristotle, *"is one in which the middle class is in control."* This is the meaning of America's greatness. This is the heart of everything American coming together in democracy. The essence of the nobility and greatness of democracy is in the words of President Franklin Roosevelt: *"Government is ourselves the voters of this country."*

The daunting challenge before us is to prevent a Republican political takeover of American democracy by a "maga" authoritarian regime, secure an American future from the want, desperation, and despair of the Republican "Trickle-Down" society, and assure the right of everyone to an honest and stable living. This is the urgent imperative of today's America as the desperation of everyday working Americans widens in the wake of the "Trickle-Down" monopoly inflationary assault on the people's cost of living.

The denial of state sponsored "Trickle-Down" human bondage in America can no longer be sustained. The ability to participate in America's prosperity in Freedom, Equality, and Justice are paramount if we are to feel the power of Liberty's promise. Most importantly, as citizens of democracy, we have duty and an obligation to follow the Truth, speak the Truth, and share the Truth.

Truth is the essence of who we are as a democratic people that empowers us as a sovereign people to be Forever Free. Freedom is Liberty's Truth. Democracy is Liberty's Trust. Equality is Liberty's Reality. Liberty is you and me walking the streets of America together in oneness regardless of who we are, the color of our skin, or where we came from. That we are the world's great "melting pot" of democracy is the nobility of what it means to be American. Our greatness is in what we represent as a united People of Liberty Forever Free in a multi-ethnic, multicultural diverse democracy of the people. Liberty calls out of the darkness for the people of

America to champion an America of generations of immigrants to a New Age of Freedom, Equality, and Justice for all.

III

The Founder's promise of Liberty, Equality, and Justice is America's affirmation of Freedom, Democracy, and Truth. This is the founding promise upon which rests the idea of an America in which government is responsible to *"promote the "General Welfare, and secure the "Blessings of Liberty to ourselves and our Prosperity."*

To secure and behold the Promise of Liberty for a just and inclusive America is the challenge before us. As Sylvia Clute notes in *Destiny Unveiled*, the task of restoration and renewal is straight forward: *"We must build a bulwark against governmental…tyranny… [and restore to America]…a Nation that…embodies Freedom… Equality…[and] the Masters Justice."* This sense of Liberty is the splendor, majesty, and glory of what Freedom represents to all the peoples of the world. It is for each of us in this American moment to pledge as a People of Liberty our faith, loyalty, and commitment to uphold and protect the Constitution of the United State against all enemies, "foreign and domestic."

What we are witnessing in this political moment is the "no holds barred" final Republican "end game" against the people of America for absolute power supremacy. In real political terms it is now the struggle for Republican power dominance to institutionalize forever the human bondage of the Republican "financialized" predatory "Trickle-Down" society of want, desperation, and despair. The everyday reality of Republican radical political extremism, white supremacy politics, unaccountable "dark money," proliferation of the "Big Lie," and the blatant incitement of sedition and insurrection to maintain political power is a testament to the reality democracy in America is under attack.

If history is any example, the Conservative political extremism political divide of the moment represents a radical turning point in the American experience. Remember it was the financiers and industrialists of central Europe in the Nineteen Thirties that funded the fascists in exchange for docile workers and big profits. Not only did the fascists on assuming power in January 1933, dismantle the nation's democracy in the first six months but outlawed the workers' unions throughout the country.

And, in similar fashion, the Republican political establishment on assuming power in 1981, **IMPLEMENTED** the Conservative "Trickle-Down" Revolution; waged war on the workers' unions of America with Right to Work Laws; **DISMANTLED** America's industrial prosperity to foreign labor, **DEREGULATED** the "rule of law" in every sector of American life; **DESTROYED** America's ability to employ its people with secure living wage jobs; and **ESTABLISHED** the Conservative predatory "survival of the fittest" economy of *"you're on your own"* America.

Not only is American democracy today broken and paralyzed from decades of Republican political greed, corruption, and polarization, the very idea of America itself is in its final death throes. Unless democracy triumphs over the darkness of fascist greed, legal corruption, and political injustice in 2024, what remains of the idea of America for future generations will not even be just an historical footnote.

This is the national nightmare of this American moment as we bear witness to a new generation of "designing men" of "big money" power corruption at the heart of the Conservative Social Darwin political-economic supremacy over America. The political reality here as we come to terms with the coming 2024 election, is as reported by *The Week* (December 2020): Republican candidates *"have lost the popular vote in seven of the past eight presidential elections, [they] have shown…[a] willingness to use any means necessary to exercise power [in] that holding power is more important than preserving America's democracy."*

We must as a People of Liberty today recognize the rise of American "fascism" for what it is, and what it represents for the future of democracy in America. As difficult as it may sound, consider we must the meaning of "radical rebellion" to comprehend the political reality of the Republican attempted violent takeover of democracy to seize absolute power. The people of America witnessed an armed violent revolutionary act causing death and destruction with the intent of political assassination. January 6, 2021. Remember this date. It will go down in the annals of the American experience as a "day of infamy," the crown jewel of fascism" in America that will forever enshrine the power of evil in our midst to destroy Democracy, Truth, and Justice.

IV

Why the Republican Insurrection conspiracy of January 6, 2021? The answer is simply *"the leader,"* as Umberto Eco so powerfully writes in *"Eternal Fascism"*: *"knowing that his power was not delegated to him democratically…also knows that his force is based on the weakness of the masses.* The political dynamic in play is really very straight forward. Fascism is inherently racist, an ideology to mask resentment and hatred that puts money and power ahead of human beings. The fanatical despotism of fascism is *"based on selective…qualitative populism. In a DEMOCRACY… citizens have individual rights [and collectively] have a political impact…[in] the decision of the majority. For FASCISM, individuals as individuals have no rights, and the people are conceived as a quantity, a monolithic entity expressing the common will… Thus, the people is a theatrical fiction."* And in that fiction there will come a future, Eco predicted, that *"a TV or Internet populism will present the emotional response of a selected group of citizens and be accepted as the Voice of the People.""*

The ultimate truth we are seeing is a reality few don't want to see, or perhaps, just don't want to believe can happen in America. The seditionists *"arrayed against American democracy,"* Chris Hedges writes in *AMERICAN FASCISTS, hate the liberal, enlightened world formed by the Constitution [and] "are waiting for a moment to strike, a national crisis that will allow them to shred the Constitution ... bent on our destruction."* And strike they did on January 6, 2021 against the people's representatives sitting in Congressional session encouraged and led by a political authoritarian demagogue bent on the destruction of the Constitution and democracy in America. *"Power is not a means,"* writes Orwell, *it's "an end," and "the consequences" of the "act are included in the act itself."*

Is not any act that seeks to encourage, abet, or condone violent insurrection to obstruct a Constitutional transfer of power considered ANARCHY? Is not any act by any person, group, or party to limit, restrict, or hinder in any way the peoples' fundamental right to vote considered a CRIMINAL ACT? Is not any act by any government official, including members of Congress, that violates his or her Oath of Office to uphold, defend, and protect the Constitution of the United States a CRIME against the sovereignty of the people?

The ensuing reality following the attempted "fascist" coup d'état on the legislative branch of American governance may distract and confuse some. But we witnessed as a people the overwhelming majority of the Republican political establishment vote to block a bipartisan "Congressional Insurrection Commission. Time nevertheless has revealed the identity of those complicit in "the biggest threat to American democracy since the Civil War," from a corrupt wannabe authoritarian tyrant to the fomenters, perpetrators, the political terrorists themselves, and certainly all the Congressional enablers having prior knowledge of the Republican plan for the violent revolutionary insurrection to overthrow an officially elected United States Government

Now Republican enablers see fit to traffic in the "big lie," falsehoods, and disinformation, but the "rule of law" gets the last word. The truth of all involved in the revolutionary insurrection can no longer be denied or white washed despite all the lies and misinformation. The face of justice in this American moment may perhaps best be described in the words of George Orwell, *"we have now sunk to a depth at which the restatement of the obvious is the first duty of intelligent men.*

Today there is no moral, legal, or Constitutional constraint the Republican political establishment won't cross in the drive to secure absolute authoritarian rule. Insurrection is the ultimate "fascist" transgression against democracy. Everyone complicit in the "Stop the Steal" Republican Conspiracy of January 6, 2021, must be identified and recorded by name for the historical record. Every official having taken an "Oath" to uphold and defend the Constitution found complicit in "sedition" must be removed from Public office pursuant to Section 3 of the XIV Amendment of the Constitution of the United States of America.

In today's political reality Democracy or Autocracy is the political agenda. Parliamentary democracy in America is "on hold" through 2024 as the Republican "maga" political establishment holds the legislative power of "NO" over the welfare of the American people. And be assured, the Republican "maga" power offensive to seize absolute power and upend America's democracy in 2024 is a 1930s racist authoritarian model of "fascism" for a 2025 America.

This could be tomorrow's America. As we witness an extremist Republican political establishment foster the "Big Lie," disinformation, and conspiracy theories to secure and maintain power supremacy, we must come to terms with the "reality" that we are a People of Liberty only a heartbeat away from becoming a draconian "right-wing" authoritarian" state. Vice President Henry Wallace in a similar time warned the American people that America's "fascists" are the "designing men" of wealth and power that seek out political power *to "keep the common man in eternal subjugation."*

The lesson of the history of "fascism" is that a functioning democracy cannot withstand the march of "right-wing" extremism where there is a failure of democracy to hold politicians accountable and control anti-democratic disinformation, hate, and fear. American democracy in this American moment is in the hands of a Republican "fascist" political cabal committed to undermine and subvert the Constitution, and grant Republicans in power the authority to negate and overturn the people's electoral mandate. Should the Republican "fascist" drive to hinder in any way the people's Constitutional fundamental right to vote, fascism will takedown the Constitutional order of the United States of America. There is no maybe here. The death of Freedom and Democracy in America, and the hold of right-wing "fascist" authoritarianism forever in the hands of "designing men" is simply a matter of time.

The Republican Fifty-Year "Assault on America" for political control of America's power and wealth has been painful, frightening and absurd beyond any rational comprehension. I find it difficult today to understand the sacrifice of my generation on so many Asian battlefields, when I consider the reality of how America's Constitutional promise and fundamental principles of democracy have been usurped by ruthless "designing men" for wealth, power, and political dominance.

Universal greed, political corruption, and the fundamental reality of "human bondage" now reign over the land of our fathers. All those days of yesterday's secure and prosperous way of life for a patriotic hardworking people are now all but a distant memory. The cornerstones of democracy have been slowly chipped away to where the Constitutional right to express the will of the people has become a tarnished Republican "fascist" political mandate to enable power dominance. All that I once cherished as an American disappeared in a political instant in 1980, and is today the Republican world of political authoritarianism, legislative tyranny, voter suppression, and violent insurrection.

Today's American political reality of want, desperation, and despair is the Republican political "secret" reality of the laissez faire "Trickle-Down" agenda to overturn democracy, concentrate the wealth of American prosperity in the financial power elite, and destroy the people's earning power and way of life. Human life has become the Republican fodder of "lives for profit" enrichment; the common good but an obstacle to overcome in the pursuit of greed, power, and wealth; life itself a luxury to be enjoyed by the financial elite at whatever the cost to democracy, to the people, to the nation.

The "Republicans against Democracy" struggle for the Soul of America threatens today to forever erase America's traditions, values, culture of truth and decency. Catherine Crier in *Patriot Acts*, discusses the political philosophy of Friedrich Hayek often lauded by key Conservative leaders in the Nineteen Eighties. She reminds us that Hayek spoke of "*how political philosophy and personality coincide and the dangers this presents to a real democracy,*" and notes "*similarities between conservatives and socialists.*" For example, the Conservatives do "*not object to coercion or arbitrary power. The Conservative believes "government … ought not to be too much restricted by rigid rules …[he's] content to expand government as long as they are in control … [and] like the socialist, he regards himself as entitled to force the values he holds on other people.*" And worthy of note, Crier observed "*that power could reside in an overreaching bureaucracy, or, even worse, might be handed to a single president by congressional decree.*" Pause here we might to ponder well the political reality of January 6, 2021 and a demonic evil political outcome in 2024.

V

Through hypocrisy, disinformation, and political deceit, radical Conservative extremism has gradually over four decades transformed America into a Republican subsistence debt-ridden casino society. This is no accident. The Republican "Pooring of America" is the political foundation of despair that has brought open parochial "fascism" into the fray for Republican political dominance. Consider the "Pooring of America" in the context of the Republican four decade triumph of the 1981 Conservative "Trickle-Down" agenda:

Political Deregulation of the "rule of law" in every sector of American life in pursuit of unhindered capital dominance over America that is today's "Trickle-Down" debt-based predatory economy, subsistence-wage living, monopolies, profiteers, climate change denial, and the concentration of America's wealth in the 1%;

Political Abandonment of America's communities to overseas labor and big profits justified by the Conservative ideological extremism of "surplus" people are *responsible for their own fate";*

Political Erosion of the ability of "representative" government to function on behalf of the "public good" in favor of the rich and the financial power elite;

Political Demise of truth, decency, and morality in the body politic through the ruthless employment of deceit, lies, disinformation, and the manipulation of democracy;

Political Suppression of state voter rights to disenfranchise millions of Americans from exercising the Constitutional right to vote, and Republican engineered state election laws to reverse the "will" of the people;

Political Incitement of division, chaos, mob violence, and bloodshed to "overturn" the "will of the people" in order to maintain power supremacy and economic domination over America.

Everywhere across the political landscape of America there reigns the dismal darkness of Republican denial of truth, alternate facts, and disinformation. And we are as a consequence a nation confronted daily with lies, confusion, and hatred. We are today by Conservative political design a confused "Trickle-Down" People of Liberty "left behind" as "surplus" remnants of democracy *"responsible for our own fate."* The Conservative ideological reality of decades of Republican political subversion of liberty, America's moral, political, and cultural norms, and the political obstruction of the "rule of law" is the political reality of "dark money" political dominance over America's Constitutional democracy. The "great storm" for the "soul of America" is upon us as "designing men" of greed and corruption endeavor to forever eradicate the promise of democracy that gives life to an America of "Liberty, Truth, and Justice.

Responsible leadership can begin and promote political change, but only through Congressional legislation can responsible change be accomplished. And as night surely turns into day, today's Republican Congressional body of "maga" radical extremism politics will not vote to support any people's initiative that will *"promote the general Welfare,"* or, advance the unity, peace, and security of the American people.

In a functional people's democracy, the essential reality of Equality and Justice is as President Franklin Roosevelt observed during the "great depression" of the1930s: *"True individual freedom cannot exist without economic security and independence; freedom means the supremacy of human rights everywhere; our unity of purpose [is] to gain those rights and keep them."*

VI

The enormity of the tragedy of America's struggle to survive the Conservative predatory juggernaut can be readily understood once we consider and fathom America has the highest "poverty rate" among the 35 Economic Cooperation and Development nations. The Conservative Social Darwin ideological *"survival of the fittest"* reality is that today an illness can bankrupt a family to a life of poverty, a college education for the average American is a guaranteed lifetime of student debt, and today's speculation-driven "bankrupt" retirees on Social Security struggle to exist a stone's throw away from life on the street.

Historically, the Republican "Trickle-Down" predatory pillage and plunder of "laissez-faire" casino capitalism have benefitted only the financial elite. Never has the "Trickle-Down" prosperity" for the few benefited the "general welfare" of the people.

Today's Republican legislated "Trickle-Down" policies are representative of the most extreme version of Social Darwin *"survival of the fittest"* economics. States political analyst Mike Lofgren, America *"ranks thirty-fifth (actually over fiftieth today) among the nations in life expectancy at birth"* and, *"in measures of economic quality, social mobility, and poverty prevention, the United States ranks twenty-seventh out of the thirty-one advanced industrial nations ..."* The economic "Trickle-Down" reality of the Republican "Profit over People" predatory agenda is an America of devastated impoverished families struggling as "surplus people" on a subsistence living.

This is the economic tragedy Professor Rana of the Cornell Law School has made so dramatically clear, writing": *"income and wealth inequality (has) dramatically increased...social stagnation is increasingly the norm...average earnings [are] barely above what they were 50 years ago, and 80 percent of the income growth of the past twenty-five years going to the top one percent.*" The Republican Forty-Year legislated "Trickle-Down" triumph of today's Conservative "free of obligations" individual extremism is the narrative of America's economic bondage.

"The silence," comments Michael Steinberger in *The Week (May 22, 2010), "is yet another indication of how warped our politics [have] become."* The political disgrace of the Conservative political indifference and tragic non-response to America's national suffering is a national shame.

In pure economic terms, all of America's economic gain over the last three decades has gone to the top, at least 50 percent of America lives in poverty or on the edge of poverty. With an annual median per capita income at some $30,000, the real average hourly wage has stagnated since 1973; millions of American workers long for a non-existent living-wage job, and most employed Americans are in real time one pay check or medical crisis away from living on the street.

The social-economic devastation of the Republican predatory Profit over People subsistence world is for every working American the narrative of a People of Liberty abandoned and forgotten as "just surplus." We are a People of Liberty reliving the reincarnation of America's Gilded Age of devastating poverty, gargantuan wealth, absolute power and privilege, while the existence of a "surplus" people in crisis is committed to spending their entire subsistence on taxes, bread, and rent.

No one in America is poor because they want to be poor. No one in America is homeless because they want be homeless. No one in America wants die because they can't afford the medical procedure that will save their life. Some 180 million Americans across America live poor, desperate, or in fear of life itself because the Republican political establishment in the 1970s chose to "dance with the devil" to transform America's competitive market economy and electoral democracy into a predatory debt-based "every man for himself" subsistence "animal farm" of unregulated unfettered profitability and wealth concentration.

The four decade Conservative political-economic assault on America for power and wealth has delivered America's worker's middle class prosperity and justice before the law over to the exploitation of the corruption of the speculators and profiteers. And these financial gurus of greed and corruption, "free of obligations," have devastated all that a People of Liberty consider to be America - be it the rule of law, legislative oversight, income equality, affordable housing, healthcare, and education, government services, and a family's right to prosper.

We have always treasured as a nation the "American family" as our most prized American value. America's hard truth today is the Republican Forty-Year assault on America's "middle class" has delivered the well-being of the American family to an institutionalized Conservative predatory "Profit over People" subsistence economy. When we ponder the crisis of the American family subsisting in today's Republican "Trickle-Down" America, may we hear the voice of Salome in *"Why Is America Suffering"*: *"The way to destroy the family is to create such deep poverty that parents, working two or three jobs to survive … lose touch with each other, and their children grow up as strangers".*

Wage poverty, human suffering, desperation, and despair are sufficient reasons we must today confront in 2024 the financial greed, legal corruption, and political injustice of America's Conservative "Profit over People" predatory "Trickle-Down" subsistence America.

The political disgrace of the Conservative political indifference and tragic non-response to America's national suffering is a national shame. This is America's Conservative "political delusion" political of who we are as a democratic people living manipulated, robbed, and broken in of a "deregulated" America once recognized as the "beacon of liberty."

The Republican *1971 grand design of the "survival of the fittest"* agenda of consolidated wealth and power is today the dismantled prosperity of America's middle class, a People of Liberty relegated to an impoverished "surplus people" struggling in the Republican subsistence "Trickle-Down" society of poverty, desperation, and despair.

DEATH OF YESTERDAY

Gone is our America of yesterday's middle class prosperity to Republican political and economic greed, corruption, and deceit

Lost is our America economically stable and secure in Liberty, Truth, and Justice to a Conservative engineered financial debt-based casino economy of the "survival of the fittest"

No more is our America the once revered "Beacon of Liberty" founded in freedom and democracy pledged to protect "the General Welfare" and the "Blessings of Liberty for Ourselves and our Posterity."

Gone is our America of the "Rule of Law" and "Justice for All," today politically deregulated to accommodate the predatory ideology of "profit over people, white supremacy politics, freedom from responsibility, and "freedom to fend for oneself" in a lawless subsistence world of "every man America for himself."

FIVE
HISTORICAL TRUTHS

President
Abraham Lincoln
"A house divided against itself cannot
stand. I believe this nation cannot
endure half slave and half free… It will
become all one thing or all the other."

The record shows that throughout history nations divided against itself are brought to destruction, and in most cases, as a direct result of an unrelenting greed for land, wealth, and power. America is a house divided, a nation embattled over Conservative lies and the disinformation of disruption that seeks to destroy American democracy in the name of unhampered capital supremacy, absolute power and concentrated wealth.

The Conservatives of ideological extremism today see themselves entitled to force the values they hold on other people to secure "unlimited government control." We see not only the Republican promulgation of the "Big Lie" since the 2020 national election, but the Covid Delta anti-vaccine disinformation that was the cause of over a million American deaths. And now we are now faced with a comprehensive Conservative attempt to "white wash" American history.

Consider we must the distasteful the reality of "white supremacy" over America from the first days of the European invasion of the Americas to the present moment. Racism is the hidden story of America from white settlement to the Civil War through Jim Crow America to the struggle for civil rights in the 1960s. Today it is the Republican racist campaign to disenfranchise the minority vote across America.

The Spanish in the 16th century conquered three empires in South America that reduced the native population from 25 million to 1.5 million. The English occupation of North America and the American "Manifest Destiny" march westward resulted in settler land grabs that forced the removal of the Amerindian population from their lands that by 1890 reduced the native American population from 12 million to less than 300,000. Who today gives pause to reflect on the blood and sacrifice of the Trail of Tears, Sand Creek, and Wounded Knee?

Who today can feel the ruthless oppression and suffering of Black Americans in America's enduring struggle to participate in "a more perfect union? In the English colonies of the 17th century, historian Abigail Swingen records *in Competing Visions of Empire, "blackness became equated with slavery, which had its starkest expression in colonial laws and codes [that] emphasized race in all matters. Race was the foundation of the social system — white skin meant freedom, domination, and power; black skin slavery, submission, and powerlessness…in a system that was based on oppressing the vast majority of the population,…of possessive individualism that valued property rights above all else…Concepts of racial difference…that never ended for those who made it to the New World."* European and American serfdom, slavery, and exploitive plantation agriculture continued as a divisive political exponent of American life to (and after) the Emancipation Proclamation of 1863.

In practical terms, the "white supremacist" narrative has prevailed from the Reconstruction Era of racial segregation through the 1960s race struggle for human rights to the present day. And today the struggle for racial equality continues with the struggle against Republican voter suppression laws that are at the heart of the Conservative ideological "racial" doctrine to disenfranchise the minority vote from inclusion in the will of the majority.

President Johnson in 1965 signed into law the Voting Rights Act, legislation that was gutted by the Republican Conservative ideological "possessive individualism" that values property, wealth, and power above all else. The political reality of racism in this American moment is the bigotry, hatred, and advocacy for white supremacy that is the personification of evil for all America.

From the structural racism of "Jim Crow" to today's mass incarceration and violence in the life of Black America, the Republican reality of "white supremacy" politics is summed up in the words of Malcolm X in the 1960s: *"You don't catch hell because you're a Mason... You catch hell because you're a black man...So we are all black people...second-class citizens...brought here by the people who came here on the "Mayflower."*

The reality of the centuries old struggle for land, wealth, and white power need not distract from the "Idea of America" envisioned by the Founding Fathers. Thomas Jefferson in 1776 drafted a clause in the Declaration of Independence condemning slavery, but was blocked by the southern slave interests over a required unanimous vote for Independence. From the beginning of the American experiment it was understood that the pursuit of Constitutional democracy of "liberty and justice for all" was a never ending struggle toward a "more perfect union." To "white wash" American history is to deny the "Idea of America" and all who sacrificed, suffered, and died in the struggle for that "more perfect union."

Every American is entitled to an honest and meaningful understanding of America's history of "race and racism" that, however uncomfortable, shaped the reality of who we are as a People of Liberty in this American moment. If we are to achieve the promise of a multiracial democracy of the world's exiles, we must address as a People of Liberty the Conservative ideological racial imperative that polarizes every aspect of American life.

The time has come we embrace together the promise our children pledge every day of an America of "liberty and justice for all." Despite the Conservative "Assault on Democracy" to achieve "white supremacy" over the body politic, the reality of who are as a People of Liberty in this American moment is captured so meaningfully by Heather McGhee, in *"The Sum of Us: We've found the enemy, and it's not each other."*

Now as I reflect on the "blessings of liberty" I've known over a lifetime, I see our uniquely American beliefs about to be politically erased, and with it the beauty and majesty of what remains of all that we as a People of Liberty hold sacred - an American democracy founded on Justice, civil liberties protected by the rule of law, every citizen's Constitutional right to vote, and the promise of a better tomorrow for all our children. With some 400 Republican voter rights suppression bills in 48 states passed or pending, all that we cherish as a free democratic people is about to be transformed into a Republican "fascist" world of systemic oppression, national misery, and the political-economic despotism of individual powerlessness. This is America's ever-present "fascist" reality staring us in the face."

A recurring Orwellian theme of totalitarianism is that "fascists" never assume power with the intention of relinquishing it. *"Are we dead,"* Orwell asks? *"Shall we meet in the place where there is no darkness?"* The answer avowed in the wisdom of President Franklin D. Roosevelt is *"democracy is not safe if the people tolerate the growth of PRIVATE POWER."* And to Republican extremists in today's America "private power" is "white power."

Understand that private power is "fascism," the political authoritarian ownership of a people by a person of iniquity or by a small radical political establishment or oligarchy. And remember we must the warning of Sinclair Lewis to America: *"when fascism comes it will be wrapped in the flag and carrying a cross."*

The final battle for America has begun. We are a country in this American moment facing the ultimate reality of political truth: authoritarian rule is the death of a nation. To recognize and resist this fundamental reality in any democracy, the question before a People of Liberty becomes, at what point does a democratic nation declare a "criminal" organization a radicalized political "party" ommitted to the violent "overthrow of democracy" to achieve and maintain power hegemony over a democratic nation?

For a People of Liberty who Pledge Allegiance to a free

Democratic Republic and a culture of "liberty and justice for all," it is an unimaginable "criminal" human tragedy to see over 180 million Americans struggling to subsist in a "fascist" world of the *"survival of the fittest"* where over a million Americans have given their "last full measure" on a thousand battlefields in the belief of an America of Freedom, Equality, and Justice Forever Free.

While Republicans have been able to unanimously vote to block legislation for infrastructure renewal, family assistance, and job initiatives to rebuild America, "people" legislation in the interest of the "common good" has shown that determined and timely government intervention is paramount to the preservation of the life of the nation.

The President's people's agenda is in every sense a one-time road to national recovery for a people where the top 1% of income earners have a greater share of household wealth than the whole of middle class America. At a cost of 1.2 percent of GDP, *The Week* (October 22, 2021) reports that the passage of the human-infrastructure "Build Back Better" recovery legislation is essential to addressing America's "alarming stagnation" and "soaring economic inequality." The legislation wouldl address care for the elderly, invest in public education, and combat climate change. "Child tax credits will lift millions of children out of poverty," reduce prescription drug bills costs for seniors, and strengthen working American families. Writes journalist Dave D'Alessandro of the Newark, N.J *Star-Ledger:* *"Every year we fail to invest in kids and education [that] leads to continuing poverty and 'decades of wasted human potential.' If we don't invest in the future, our future will be grim."*

As America's national "democratic" recovery effort progresses after decades of Republican predatory "Trickle-Down" destruction, the challenge before us must focus on the resolve, resilience, and perseverance of Truth, Democracy, and Justice as we unite to usher in a new era of "Liberty, Equality, and Justice for all."

M.G. Montpelier

A WORLD DEFILED

I feel the raging fury of
betrayal and corruption
ravaging a world defiled

I weep for the many struggling
the desperation of unchecked
climate destruction

I behold with compassion
A planet longing for clean
energy in a burning world

SIX

WORLD ON FIRE

"Climate change is one of the gravest crisis our planet has ever faced." The "most important lawsuit on the planet" was filed in 2015 in the U.S. District Court of Eugene, Oregon. The federal court judge ruled the case to go forward, saying: *"I have no doubt that to a right to a climate system capable of sustaining human life is fundamental to a free and ordered society."* Public trust rights *"both predated the Constitution and are secured by it, and can't be "legislated away."*

David Russell
Horsemen of the Apocalypse

MONDAY, AUGUST 30, 2023

In the quiet of late evening, Bill and Martha relax in quiet conversation on the latest destructive disaster of an America in permanent political-economic crisis.

With a blank expression of foreboding, Bill asks, "What's that line, 'water, water everywhere'? Martha, seeing Bill is anxiously pondering the day's consequences of the unrelenting

Conservative denial of Climate Change, says "that would be Samuel Taylor Coleridge's *The Ancient Mariner, "Water Water everywhere not a drop to drink."* Perhaps the plight we may all face in the very near future. Why do you ask?"

"Just a lingering thought. Martha, on the latest catastrophic flooding along the East and Gulf Coasts: "water everywhere," billion dollar infrastructure devastation, and the loss of power for over a million people. I'm afraid, Martha, this is the new normal for humanity and the planet. Climate change and environmental disaster is here, and it's hitting hard this year everywhere across the planet.

"The Conservative apologists of political "you're on your own" extremism don't want to hear the oceans are warming, or the world's glaciers are disappearing as a consequence of global carbon pollution. And they even refuse to acknowledge the Climate Change reality that each new year is becoming the hottest year on record. Devastating hurricanes, typhoons, droughts, flooding, firestorms, and earthquakes are raining havoc and destruction on every continent. Seventy percent of the planet's forests have been cut down, altering the ecological balance of the Earth, eight million animal and plant species on the planet are on the threshold of extinction, and Planet Earth is projected to be on the road to environmental collapse by 2050.

"The global climate apocalypse of destruction, Martha, is the carbon energy reality before us as we continue to produce over 85 billion tons of carbon emissions annually. Sea levels are rising; power grids overwhelmed; water reservoirs depleted; infrastructure burning. The last eight years have been the warmest on record. The 2021 heat wave broke record highs in South America, the United States, Canada, England, Europe, and Asia. The decade-long mega drought in America's Southwest is on a path to be the worst in 1,200 years. The catastrophic flooding in Germany, Turkey, and China is the worst in a century.

And now Martha, I see in *The Week* (December 8, 2023) reports that *"November 17, 2023…was the first day in human history when the average global temperature hit 2 degrees Celsius warmer than pre-industrial levels…Every month since June has set a new high temperature…Earth is speeding toward 2.5 to 2.9 degrees Celsius of warming by the end of the century."*

Time is running out for Planet Earth as the Republican "dark money" anti-climate profit agenda continues to block Congressional action to fund Global Warming control through a measured public policy that would transform America's fossil fuel dependency to a 21ˢᵗ Century American Renewable Clean Energy Infrastructure. The climate change crisis of global carbon pollution is for a burning world the most deplorable Lives for Profit "collateral damage" event in uman history. As the planet heats up destroying lives, property, and infrastructure, America's Republican *"survival t fittest"* fossil fuel gurus of climate change denial and "dark money" politics have politically rolled-back America's environmental protections, abandoned climate change agreements, and blocked cheap renewable energy initiatives.

"I understand, Bill. But through the political control of power corruption, the Conservative laissez-faire political extremists have been able to TRANSFORM our once national economic prosperity into a profit apocalypse of impoverished serfdom, hunger, and want; FOSTER a violent insurrection to overturn America's democratic electoral process to maintain power; DISENFRANCHISE millions of citizens from their Constitution right to vote; and REORDER with impunity a national pandemic into a Republican political homicidal apocalypse of the unvaccinated approaching over a million deaths. That begs the political reality before us in 2022: Can our battered democratic institutions protect the people's Constitutional safeguards designed to defend America's democracy from enemies not only "foreign," but enemies "domestic?"

The challenge of Climate Change destruction is as you often fume, Bill, the story of politically protected profit over planetary sustainability. Despite the annual increase of catastrophic climate events throughout the world in number, frequency, and intensity, the "big money" power brokers of climate change denial control the politics of unhindered vulture capitalism, climate change legislation, and clean energy.

"I would say that sums up the reality of the Conservative authoritarian "dark money" politics of the *"survival of the fittest"* capital supremacy in America, Martha. America's Conservative environmental reality is the destruction of the planet to satisfy an insatiable craving for wealth and profit over human life itself. It's the Republican Fifty-Year laissez-faire extremism of "Profit over People" at whatever the cost to humanity and the environment all over again.

"Just follow the money, Martha. Wealth and profit are at the heart of the political debate over the cost of the President's national "human-infrastructure" package to bring the working people of America into the 21st Century. It's not about the "cost effectiveness" of giving people dignity and an honorable existence, the legislation for the "common good" ll pay for itself once the wealthy and corporations begin to pay their fair share. Conservative climate Change denial and "big money" power is blocking a people's initiative for reducing the carbon blueprint and clean energy renewal. It's about the right to access affordable drug prices, and the financial power restricting the means for giving a People of Liberty hope to live without struggle and suffering. It is about protecting the profits, wealth, and privilege of the financial power elite working to prevent "sweeping historical changes" that will mandate the Ultra-Rich pay something instead of nothing and, for once in 50 years, strengthen low-income and middle-class working families with child care, education, and child poverty support, and grow good living-wage jobs in a de-industrialized desert society of financial greed.

"I know. I know, Bill. But this is our Conservative ideological *"survival of the fittest"* political-economic reality. Even though "73% of Americans support policies to cut greenhouse gas emissions in half by 2030," the destructive political power of greed and corruption holds us and our planetary world hostage to unfettered "laissez-faire" climate exploitation.

"Well, 'it's not over 'til it's over,' Bill. There's no alternative to mankind's reconciliation with creation. This will all be over one day. No more tears, no more suffering, no more pain. Light will emerge from the darkness and our fading democracy will be transformed again into a land of the living. Greed and corruption will be swallowed up in victory. And the sting of death that now engulfs the people of America will be no more.

In our quest for Liberty, Democracy, and Freedom, Bill, we *"have it in our power to begin the world over again."* "Actually, it's quite simple, Bill. Political change for the survival of the common good and the future of the planet comes down to who we vote for: an Autocracy of Exploitation or a Democracy of the People!"

Look around
Children of the Earth,
The planet mourns,
"as the Land lies polluted,
defiled by its inhabitants
who have transgressed the
laws...a curse consumes the
land and its people burn."
Hosea

PEACE WE SAY

**"PEACE" Say We
to the
Power Brokers of
Greed**

**"PEACE" Say We
to the
Merchants of
Death**

**"PEACE" Say We
to the
Predatory Wars of
Human Suffering**

SEVEN

FOREVER WARS

"The mystic chords of memory, stretching from every battlefield and patriot gave to every living heart and hearthstone all over this broad land, will yet swell the chorus of the Union, when again touched, assurely they will be, by the better angels of our nature."
Abraham Lincoln
First Inaugural Address, 1861

Sunday Evening

Bill, rising from his chair before the television with a sigh of disgust mutters to himself, "The 20-year $300 million a day Afghan War is finally over. But is the golden goose that never stops giving really dead?"

"What's that? Martha calls out... Walking into the sitting room with a smile, she asks, "What was that all about?"

"I was just commenting to myself on the fall of Afghanistan, Martha. We've ventured to engage in a twenty year military economic deployment in Asia, Africa, and the Middle East on a "credit card." That has involved six wars, and all that remains are the remnants of "delusion and dishonesty," over a million dead, countries destroyed, displacement and hunger as 37 million displaced human beings flee the chaos of devastation and destruction. And, of course, there's the $8 trillion war debt with over $2 trillion in interest that will never be paid off in our lifetime."

"Is there something I'm missing here, Bill?" Martha asks. "Not really, Martha," Bill responds. "I just can't seem to shake the idea that since 1945, we've maintained a permanent war economy that consumes the lion share of the federal budget, engaged in 15 military interventions over the last 42 years, and whenever a "petty dictator" or "Jihadist" flexes a muscle, the Conservative politicians, foreign policy groups, and political action committees, backed by right-wing money and influence, agitate for intervention.

"The 20-year Afghan War is no different than the Vietnam War triggered over a dubious incident, the Iraq debacle waged over weapons of mass destruction that didn't exist, and so many tragic interventions of imperial overreach. And after a year or so, the conflict becomes a "forever war" no one can explain that in the end benefits only the "flag waving" political "war profiteers" and the coffers of the financial-industrial complex. Already, the political flag of righteousness is flying anew for war. There are now politicians already heralding a coming need for a second intervention in Afghanistan. It never ends Martha, power and profit at whatever the cost marches on to the tune of deceit and destruction just as the prophet Ezekiel of long ago proclaimed, *"They have seduced my people, saying, "Peace!" when there is no peace."*

"Well, Bill, what it comes down to as George Orwell makes clear, "War is not to be won. It is meant to be continuous." I would think what it really comes down to in a democracy is who the people vote for, the candidate who values people over profit and a sense of humanity, or those who advocate the Conservative *"survival of the fittest"* extremism of unhampered vulture capitalism at any cost.

"Yes, Martha, that's the answer for a democratic people FREE of unaccountable "dark money" politics that has within its grip the ability to control the people's destiny and the future of American democracy. But think about it for a moment.

"War is something we rarely talk about unless there is an incident somewhere in the world involving the loss of American lives. War is the least discussed topic in American politics. No one is willing to acknowledge the business of war is the most profitable business of unrestricted capital supremacy.

"Actually, Martha, I see the real reason we pulled out of Afghanistan is we are simply a bankrupt nation. The unhampered supremacy of capital has destroyed America and the promise of democracy. The American empire is in its death throes. America's hegemony over global profits can no longer be sustained. The inflated dollar, massive borrowing, and rising federal deficits over the last five decades that have funded America's informal imperial expansion around the world has come to an end. Decades of waging war on a credit card, trillion dollar bank bailouts, decades of recurring wealthy tax cuts that didn't pay for themselves, billions in annual corporate subsidies, printing money at will, and our casino economic system have all contributed to America's decline since the 1981 Republican "Trickle-Down" Revolution of deregulation and private wealth creation, and today's $30 trillion national debt primarily driven by Republican political malfeasance.

This all becomes relevant when we understand America's wealth today is concentrated in the top 1 percent that owns more wealth than the entire middle class. The wealthiest among us and the richest corporations pay little to no taxes, while over two-thirds of everyday working Americans subsist on a low-wage income of which over 90 percent goes to taxes, food, and rent. You would think with the trillions of dollars we spend on killing people, we could find the money to help America's "Trickle-Down" left behind.

"The fiscal reality of America is we're broke, Martha. And that's not just you and me and the neighbor next door. America is broke. We just can't sustain trillion dollar tax cuts, extravagant wealthy entitlements, and billions in corporate subsidies any longer without massive borrowing. All this business of war seems to be as John Lanchester observed recently in the *London Review of Books, 'We have in effect had to declare war to get us out of the hole created by our economic system."*

"I know, Bill. But I find this all disgustingly pathetic, repulsive, and disheartening. I just don't see any legitimacy in conflicts of death and destruction waged in our name to make the world safe for profiteering. The hard truth of American politics is that the vast majority of the American people neither grasps nor subscribes to the flagrant corruption and manipulation of the politics of exploitation that has so oppressed and demoralized the people of America. In fact, most Americans show little concern for day-to-day policy issues and are prone to accept party line disinformation. The triumph of greed at any cost is just not who we are, Bill, or what the Framers intended for an America founded on the idea of Liberty, Truth, and Justice.

"What we are witnessing at home and around the world is a catastrophic human apocalypse involving millions of human beings struggling to survive hunger, forced migration, and political repression. And this, in one way or another, is the unfortunate tragic consequence of our domestic politics of greed, decades of foreign policy failures, and forever-wars of profit, death, and destruction.

When I look in the mirror, Bill, I see the distant quagmires of Vietnam, Afghanistan, and Iraq, and an America of bankrupt impoverished communities, their people made surplus and destitute in the quest for profit. I see the reflection of an

America in crisis, an America broken, lonely, and hurting, and a struggling "Trickle-Down" people who understand the frailty of just being human in an unjust predatory world of reckless greed, shameless corruption, and political betrayal. But most of all, Bill, I see we are still a People of Liberty who cherish from the innermost depths of our being the inviolability of an American democracy that protects and defends for one and all 'the Blessings of Liberty.'

"While reading *The Week* news the other day, I came across a report that cited '85% of Americans when surveyed declared themselves to be Christian.' And I felt at that moment the fundamental 'essence of being' that is the love Chris Hedges writes so powerfully in *The World As It Is*. That the 'essence of being" is a love that embodies what freedom and democracy are meant to represent. A love that recognizes the *'sanctity of all human beings...allows us to embrace and cherish life... to cope with inevitable despair and suffering in the healing solidarity of kindness, compassion, and self-sacrifice...resist in our nature what we know we must resist and affirm what we know we must affirm...* acknowledge that to *love another as one loves oneself is to love the universal self that unites us all...gives us meaning that endures...and alone can save us, especially from ourselves.'*

"American Exceptionalism, Bill, means to me we are a People of Liberty gathered in the world's greatest melting pot of democratic freedom, a nation of 'malice toward none' that out of the many we are one united in a lasting social order that itself bears witness to America's founding values of Liberty, Truth, and Justice. This is what the Founders meant we must become in the pursuit of 'a more perfect union,' a People of Liberty sharing values in a nation that embodies the meaning of democracy in an America dedicated to 'Liberty and Justice for All.'

"Today, Bill, everywhere we look, we bear witness to the reality we are a "Trickle-Down" People of Liberty stranded in a Republican desert of want, desperation, and despair. Nevertheless, despite all our flaws, Bill, and all the political injustices carried out by the power brokers in our name, we are a resolute people constitutionally committed "In God We Trust" to an America of Democracy, Truth, and Justice.

"These are troubled times that endeavor to radicalize and blind the uninformed to the Republican campaign of lies, disinformation, and deceit that only subverts the essence of American freedom and democracy. The tyranny of wealth and power of "designing men" today threatens forever all we hold sacred as a People of Liberty. One day the darkness of greed and corruption that seeks to eliminate the "Blessings of Liberty" will be over. It is now for all who celebrate Liberty in America's "darkest hour" to give hope to those who have none.

"'*Courage,*' the Roman playwright Plautus reminds us, '*is what preserves our liberty, safety, life, and homes and parents, our country and children.*' As a People of Liberty we must stand firm in truth, embrace the freedom of our fathers, and be strong and courageous for an America 'Forever Free.'

"This, Bill, is our only hope for America, not just today, but for an America 'Forever Free' for all generations to come."

The biggest **war profiteer US**

61% of global arms sales in 2019 come from the US

5 of world's 10 largest defense contractors come from the US

57% of total arms sales by the world's 100 largest defense contractors are from the US

$6.4 trillion has been spent on the post-911 wars and conflicts in more than 80 countries, most of which was transferred to the top 5 contractors

$2.31 trillion spent on the Afghanistan War

87% **$2.02 trillion** went to the top 5 defense contractors

From 2001 to 2021, the stocks of these top five contractors outperformed the stock market overall by **58%**

$10,000 invested in an S&P 500 index fund in Sep 2001 would now be worth **$61,613**

$10,000 invested evenly in the top 5 defense contractors would now be worth **$97,295**

$10,000 invested in Lockheed Martin would now be worth **$133,559.21**

Around **380** high-ranking officials had become government lobbyists, defense contractor consultants or board members and executives within two years of leaving the military between 2008 and 2018

51 members of Congress and their spouses own between $2.3 and $5.8 million worth of stocks in companies that are among world's top 30 defense contractors

Nearly **1/3** of the senate members of the Defense Subcommittee of the Appropriations Committee own stocks of top defense contractors

Sources: media reports
Graphics: Deng Zijun/GT

M.G. Montpelier

QUIET DESPERATION

TODAY I face the uncertainty
Of a suffering people living
In "Quiet Desperation"

TODAY I endure the misery
Of "Trickle-Down"
Poverty and Despair

TODAY I struggle to survive
The betrayal of
Conservative Extremism

TODAY I know this day
May be my everyday
For all my tomorrows

EIGHT
DESPERATE LIVES

Early Morning

Frank looks over at Mary, "You're not saying much this morning, Mary?" Mary, pale and visibly tired, says, "Well, I'm here. What can I say? I'm working three jobs for nickels and dimes. My girls are sick without adequate medical care. And I'm never sure we're going to make it to month's end."

Jen speaks up with an air of assuredness. "Something's got to give you guys! All there is here is crumbling roads, rusting factories, discount strip malls, franchise restaurants, box stores, and abandoned people "responsible for their own fate." And "white nationalist" Republican politicians block any productive meaningful proposal that will benefit the common good. That is, of course, except for the grift, tax cuts, and subsidies for the common good of the top one percent.

Bob breaks in, "Here she goes again. She's frustrated because she reads too much." "Actually," Frank rejoins, "she is in fact more often right than not." Jen, excited now, looks at Bob, and begins, "Bob, you just don't get it. You just don't want to hear the truth. All you listen to is conspiracy theories, disinformation, and the politics of individual extremism that enable poverty, forever debt, death care, and like my former neighbors, old age on the streets.

All began to speak at once. "OK guys!" Frank says. "Just what do you feel is the truth, Jen?" Jen, with a hard look on her face, says pointedly, "After decades of Republican "trickle-down" lies and deceit there's simply nothing left. Downtown America is an empty shell. Small business ownership barely exists. Extreme wealth owns everything. Regulatory restraint and accountability are dead. Catastrophic climate change devastation is here. Our secure living-wage jobs have gone south. Old age pension security for the elderly is gone! And the Republicans relentlessly pursue the destruction of the democratic state and their "survival of the fittest" ideological obsession to privatize Social Security, Medicare, and public education, and eliminate child labor prohibitions and minimum wage laws.

"Look around you. It gets worse. Costs continue to rise without wage relief. People are hurting. Families are struggling. Children are hungry. The struggle to maintain a decent place to live has become an everyday reality. Nobody really has anything but cheap toys. There is little to no opportunity for our children to work for a better life. And homelessness across America has become the people's scourge of America's 21st Century.

Who remembers today the Republicans of 2017 embraced white supremacy paranoia and extreme political divisiveness, enacted a trillion dollar wealthy tax cut, added $8 trillion to the Federal Deficit? Who among us took issue with the Constitutional lawlessness of 2021 when the Republicans passed nationwide racial state voter suppression laws, blocked a self-funded $3.5 trillion national human and physical infrastructure package to address poverty, good paying jobs, roads and bridges, child care, housing, and climate change-renewable energy initiatives to "Build Back Better" an America for all the people? Who this year stood up to condemn the horror of the "unanimous" Republican anti-constitutional opposition to the passage of the National Voting Rights Act to save American democracy from the hypocrisy of fascism? Sadly, the answer is staring us in the face as we, a People of Liberty, bear witness to the everyday inequality and injustices of the Republican "Trickle-Down Society of want, desperation, and despair.

"OK, Jen, so what's the answer, Bob asks? I know you guys don't want to talk politics," Jan responds, "but the first step is to acknowledge the Republican political reality for what it is. Then and only then can we begin to bring about change." Everybody nods in somewhat agreement.

"The truth is," Jen continues without so much as a breath, "we each bear in our own way the political human bondage of the Republican "Trickle-Down" economy of shame: insecure work, service jobs, pauper wages, unaffordable healthcare, housing, and education, and a subsistence standard of living. Think about it for a moment, rampant gun violence dominates our lives, opportunity for our children's future is all but non-existent, legalized financial corruption has control over the economy, and the nation's wealth and economic growth goes to the 1%. We see every day the Republican racial extremism of "Jim Crow" racial oppression, intimidation, and the denial of every American's Constitutional right to vote. Face it, the people's America of the "Land of the Free" is a wholly owned subsidiary of the financial power elite controlled through Conservative "dark money," and dominated by an authoritarian political establishment of legislative obstruction, and the spread of Republican lies, disinformation, and deceit.

Now, if we are really serious about restoring the "Land of the Free" to a democracy "of the people," we must today call out as a People of Liberty the reality of the REPUBLICAN Conservative CULTURE OF DEATH: climate change "denial" as an expedient of the Politics of Profit over Human Existence is

ENVIRONMENTAL GENOCIDE; the dissemination of Covid anti-vaccine lies and disinformation as an expression of radical ideological extremism is a POLITICAL MANSLAUGHTER; the proliferation of lies, disinformation, and deceit to undermine Constitutional democracy is POLITICAL LIBEL; "white supremacist" hate speech and racial injustice in a democracy in today's context is what Hannah Arendt referred to as "THE BANALITY OF EVIL;" "Profit over People" debt-based subsistence economics is state sponsored MEDIEVAL SERFDOM; hidden "dark money" electoral dominance is politically authorized STATE FASCISM; Republican state "voter suppression" laws and state election appointees authorized to overturn the "will" of the people is criminal ELECTORAL SUBVERSION; and the obstruction of Constitutional governance, be it executive or legislative, is unadorned criminal POLITICAL TYRANNY. And, let's be clear, the reality of a violent political insurrection coup attempt to overthrow the government in any country, whether successful or not, is for all involved regardless of status, position, or influence, what it has always been since time immemorial: "TREASON!"

Face it people, we are a People of Liberty who've been transformed by decades of Conservative power dominance from a 1970s industrial nation of "prosperity for all" to a 1980s Republican Financialized "Trickle-Down" Society of the "survival of the fittest," to the Pooring of America, to the collapse of a once prosperous middle-class. The nation is polarized and divided, public values and morality have withered, and now, in this American moment, we are a People of Liberty living the reality of an unstable politically compromised democracy on the verge of disintegration. The Republican 1971 offensive of political "betrayal" of America to "save capitalism from democracy" is today a Conservative America of subsistence wages, unaffordable cost of living, and an abandoned "surplus" democratic people struggling to survive the "fascist" onslaught of "dark money" corruption in America's political discourse.

So, in answer to your question, Bob, the solution to greed and corruption in American politics is very straight forward: Public Accountability Laws that ensure the unencumbered universal right to vote (and the assurance all votes will be counted without partisan interference); campaign "dark money" financing reform; and the return of Federal oversight over business, finance, and politics. Given today's tragic reality of disinformation, lies, and deceit in the body politic, political parties, politicians, and broadcasters must be held responsible under penalty of law for the veracity of truth. Free speech doesn't give anyone in a democracy the right to destroy or to malign, disparage, or defame, regardless who is in power.

The time has come that we must address as a People of Liberty the "Banality of Evil" in our midst. Freedom is the Constitutional Right to Vote. Every citizen's vote is the Life Blood of American democracy. I would think even you, Bob, would acknowledge that any "extremist" party that advocates racial supremacy, voter suppression, electoral subversion, elector certification fraud, violent insurrection, subsistence-wage servitude, and the "deregulation" of laws that assure a fair and just society is a "criminal organization."

If "We the People" are to once again prosper in a secure stable democracy of Liberty, Truth, and Justice, President Theodore Roosevelt reminds us that we, as a People of Liberty, *"have the right, the power, and the duty to protect [ourselves] and [our] own welfare"* from the servitude of "human bondage."

Frank, looking at his watch with a smile, stands to announce, "OK everybody, it's time to go."

II

America's Profit over People predatory "Trickle-Down" economy of wealthy tax elimination, big business "zero" taxation, subsistence-wage jobs, Lives for Profit healthcare, and middle class retirement poverty has impoverished well over 180 million Americans of today's Republican political-economic world of "individual extremism."

The reason, as previously discussed, is the Conservative political-economic supremacy over America's electoral democracy, achieved by the "political economy" theories of Buchanan, Friedman, and Bork, the Powell strategic grand design *to "save capitalism against democracy,"* and two Conservative Supreme Court "dark money" rulings.

As a consequence of Supreme Court rulings in *Buckley 1976 and Citizens United 2010*), the triumph of the Republican "Trickle-Down" agenda through aggressive "big money" vested interest financing, empty promises, and political disinformation, the Conservative "big money" political initiative in the end delivered the demise of the America's competitive market economy and the making of the Republican predatory Lives for Profit subsistence "Trickle-Down" *"survival of the fittest* "America.

The political-economic reality of the Fifty-Year Republican campaign to "save capitalism from democracy" is an America of wealth creation for a few, and for everybody else lives of economic bondage, desperation, and despair in an America lacking economic security, livable wages, safe working conditions, affordable healthcare, and society safe to raise a family.

The 1971 Powell strategic political grand design for achieving Republican political dominance over the American people achieved in the 1980s and the the making of America's financialized debt-based economy of "Profit over People" ideological extremism advanced by the American political-economic academics Buchanan, Friedman, and Bork. But the underlying political reality of the Republican political-economic "Trickle-Down" revolution has been the transformation of American democracy into a Conservative impoverished world of rusting factories, economic servitude, political moral depravity, and unhampered capital supremacy. The Conservative ideological extremism of absolute power and wealth creation is today's America.

We are as Chris Hedges observes in *The World As It Is*, an America of "unchecked greed" in which every working person struggles to survive the Conservative playground of exploitation and profit that sees **"EVERYTHING FROM HUMAN BEINGS TO THE NATURAL ENVIRONMENT AS EXPLOITABLE COMMODITIES."**

III

The term "Trickle-Down Prosperity" lays bare the privatized "political economy" of human bondage in today's Conservative *"every man for himself"* America of a democratic peoples' lost labor, property, and freedom.

The" political economy" of "Trickle-Down" poverty is the political-economic narrative of the today's America. When the financial barons and mercantile monopolies realized they had no other worlds to conquer, the financiers, profiteers and speculators in their quest for profits, plundered the national wealth, worker's wages, and the personal assets of their own people. When the politically engineered thievery and abject poverty of America comes home to roost and the financial house of cards comes crashing down from financial growth gimmicks, market manipulation, trader speculation, and corporate raiders, we see the bubbles burst, the market's collapse, and massive widespread financial disaster resulting in bank runs, depression, and massive unemployment as in the great stock market crashes through 1929 and 2008.

The political-economic dynamic in each era of greed, corruption, and injustice follows a familiar pattern: early growth and wealth accumulation, financial "laissez-faire" entitlements, accrual of investment "hot" money from wealthy tax cuts and deregulation, company megamergers, monopolistic control of the economy, transfer of middle class wealth to the superrich, and massive unrestrained speculation followed by an unsound economy, and economic collapse.

Millions of Americans become unemployed, homeless, and hungry. In the final draw, the massed wealth of the private investment schemes, financial roulette, and political maneuvers of the "big money" power brokers is concentrated in the hands of the one percent protected by government legislated taxpayer bailouts, all at the expense of the nation's political betrayal, impoverishment, and a surplus people abandoned and left to their own fate.

In *The Surplus American*, Derber and Magrass examine the fundamentals of the ideological basis of laissez-faire "political economy" to our understanding of the political philosophy of today's Republican "big money" political establishment in the "Pooring of America." The Social Darwin laissez-faire "Trickle-Down" Doctrine of the *"survivalist of the fittest"* explains the reality of the "desperate lives" of this American moment:

First, *"Everyone (is) entitled to an equal opportunity to prove their merit on the market. Those who (fail) deserve their fate ..."* (and) "nobody owes you nothin." Laissez-faire democracy offers individual FREEDOM ... *"Freedom from a network of obligations, Freedom to fend for yourself; but also Freedom to become surplus, and Freedom to starve.*

Secondly, and the crux of today's desperation and despair across America, *"suffering, even deaths, among the poor (are) part of a natural winnowing process necessary to separate the worthy from the unworthy ... misery and mortality for the worthy (are) a necessary cost for creating unprecedented prosperity: (and for the "surplus" population, "the starving vagabond," "parasites and freeloaders," just ship them off to the forced labor "surplus people detention centers."*

The predatory Conservative *"every man for himself"* America is today the political triumph of the Republican decades-long "deregulation" offensive of market manipulation, financial growth gimmicks, and the demise of middle class America. However politically disguised, it is the cornerstone reality of the Republican *"survival of the fittest"* ideological purity of Conservative Social Darwin political-economic supremacy.

IV

The Republican political triumph of 1980, 1994, 2010 provided the power base for the Republican political establishment to freely engage in a concentrated assault on the middle class economy through the enactment of the Republican laissez-faire "Trickle-Down" economic agenda: unfettered unaccountable markets, deregulation of the economy, and the destruction of America's competitive community-based industrial economy to a predatory consumer debt-based wilderness of monopolists, profiteers and financial speculators.

The Republican "deregulation" of America's competitive free market economy championed by Milton Friedman's "myth" of uncontrolled self-adjusting free markets paved the way for an America of rusting factories, bankrupt communities, and the predatory financialized consumer debt-based economy of part-time subsistence wage labor. The Republican abandonment of the Sherman Antitrust Act through the revision or abandonment of America's anti-trust regulations provided the capstone for the triumph of the Bork Doctrine to "allow firms to achieve available efficiencies through mergers without interference."

With the Republican legislated "deregulation" of government accountability oversight of the financial industry and subsequent repeal of the Glass-Steagall Act of 1935, the people of America lost all consumer and banking protection from the investment profiteers of financial growth gimmicks, and the derivatives speculation debacle that facilitated the 2007 great housing-bubble meltdown and the "2008 Financial Collapse". And it was the Republican legislated "deregulation" of the finance industry that provided the trigger for America's "financial collapse" that wiped-out millions of jobs, people's life savings, America's retirement pension accounts, and millions of home owners to foreclosure fraud, while the moneylenders, speculators, and profiteers were protected from criminal prosecution and received taxpayer funded trillion dollar government bailouts.

V

It should come as no surprise that over half of the population of America anguishes everyday on why their children are hungry, why they are working two and three jobs and still can't get a head of their situation. Every American should be asking how it is, as a People of Liberty, good people in the richest country in the world are caught up in a political quagmire of want, desperation, and despair, fleeced of yesterday's opportunities to prosper, and struggle ever day of their lives in a Conservative engineered Lives for Profit predatory "Trickle-Down" subsistence economy. In pure economic terms, all of America's economic gain over the last three decades has gone to the top, over 50% of America lives in poverty, on the edge of poverty, or just homeless. With an annual median per capita income at some $30,000, the real average hourly wage has stagnated since 1973; millions of American workers long for a non-existent living-wage job, and most employed Americans are in real time one pay check or medical crisis away from living on the street.

More than 95 percent of America's wealth is concentrated in the top 1 percent. Today the super-wealth of America is actually concentrated in the top one-tenth of the 1 percent. Might we keep in mind, three people today own more wealth than the bottom 50 percent of America while a few hundred families own just about everything else.

Economic stagnation, family consumer debt, and "forever" student debt is America's national institutional norm in the Republican unregulated Profit over People predatory debt-based economy of some 13 trillion dollars in consumer debt, including 1.5 trillion dollars in forever student debt. In 2019 as America's overall debt rose to 102% of GDP, the national debt exceeded $22 billion principally due to wealthy trillion dollar tax cuts, moneylender speculation bailouts, and 20 years of unending credit card funded foreign wars.

An impoverished America of 180 million urban and rural working poor struggle with the basic necessities of life. Average earnings for the American worker are barely what they were 50 years ago while the median annual income for two income households remains stagnant at some $58,000, two out of three working Americans earn less than a living wage, while 75 percent of Americans live paycheck to paycheck never knowing the next paycheck will be the last. Two-thirds of the American people have less than $1,000 in savings, while 44 percent of Americans don't have $400 in available cash for an emergency. Ten million Americans can't access the banking system are the "Trickle-Down" fodder of the predatory loan-shark pay day lenders that prey on the working poor.

The average America worker lives on a subsistence income with monthly expenditures of $1300 to $2000 for rent, $1200 in child care, in addition to outrageous "inflated" monopoly food, medicine, and transportation costs. And now in 2023 we find middle income families faced with "a cost of living crisis" from ballooning rents, sky-rocketing child care, spiraling personal healthcare fees, and prohibitive educational debt struggle. This is all taking place as America's financial institutions individually gross more than $40 billion in annual profits from consumer credit and big business tax cuts, while the Ultra-Rich an two-thirds of America's top corporations pay no federal income tax.

Certainly food is the basic human need. Since the advent of the Republican "Trickle-Down" Revolution of the 1980s, homelessness, hunger, and malnutrition have mushroomed across America as America's factories closed and American jobs disappeared to low-wage countries, and Americans subsisted under Conservative Social Darwin ideological policies to maximize profits. And in the richest country in the world, over 50 million Americans in this American moment live hungry, and another 20 million Americans live malnourished. Some 20 percent of America's children go to bed hungry and one in two children in their childhood years need food assistance to alleviate nutritional depravation.

The rise in hunger, from 20 million in 1980 to over 50 million Americans today, has risen dramatically under decades of Republican *"survival of the fittest"* Social Darwin food policies, temporary work, and subsistence wages. Over 50 percent of the population is bankrupt and impoverished communities across America are forced exist with food insecurity.

The Conservative ideology of the *"freedom to starve"* doesn't allow for Republican "individual freedom" politics to address food deprivation and child hunger that will ensure every American has enough to eat. Everyone has the right to starve is basic Republican ideological individual extremism. But, of course, the money is always there for trillion dollar foreign wars, trillion dollar bank bailouts, and recurring trillion dollar wealthy tax cuts, but nothing for bipartisan legislation that will provide something for the "surplus" unworthy forgotten in the impoverished America of this American moment.

Since the 1964, the electoral platform of Barry Goldwater to make Social Security voluntary to the Bush administration's push to privatized Social Security accounts, the Republican political establishment has and is presently relentlessly and ruthlessly pursuing the Conservative *"every man for himself"* core agenda for the *political elimination* of the people's medical Affordable Care Act, Social Security, Medicare and Medicaid. Might we ask ourselves in this decisive electoral moment of 2024, *what will we become as a free democratic people* in 2025 in the face of recurring Republican wealthy tax cuts and the political demise of America's human infrastructure in a Republican "fascist" autocratic world of absolute power. The election of 2024 will decide forever what remains of America's social safety net, and the Republican transfer of the America's three trillion dollar Social Security Trust Fund to the privatization of the financial sector.

Every voter remember, once the Republicans have legislatively abolished the Affordable Care Act, Social Security, Medicare and Medicaid, *"You're on your own"* as just *"surplus" in an American Conservative world of the "survival of the fittest."*

Late Afternoon

Your teen age daughter, Lacy, is involved in an automobile accident and rushed to the hospital. As you enter the emergency room, the attending physician walks over to you and says, "I'm sorry madam, but we are unable to treat your daughter. We have been advised that you have no health insurance coverage. I'm sure you can understand this medical facility is a Free Market "For-Profit" Enterprise. Unless you are in a position to make a "cash payment" at this time, I'm afraid there's nothing we can do for your daughter. Actually, it's a miracle she made it this far. You see, she didn't 'by law' have any Authorized Private Medical ID on her person at the time of the accident, and technically, should not have been transported to this clinic. I'm sorry, but only cash payment or private insurance coverage for medical care is the law of the land. Please call our Patient Processing Center tomorrow for final arrangements and any outstanding fee adjustments.

TO BEGIN ANEW

I SEE the
Torch of Liberty
Beckoning a proud
Democratic people to a
NEW AGE OF REEDOM

I HEAR the sound
Of distant drums
Echoing Freedom's
Call To LIBERTY AND
JUSTICE FOR ALL

I HEAR
The toll of
LIBERTY'S BELL
Ringing for a great
PATRIOTIC RENEWAL

I HEAR above
The din of battle
The Soul of America
Cry out to the
American Spirit:

"FEAR NOT AMERICA,
The Light of a New
Dawn Beckons to
Brighten Your Tomorrow

NINE

BEYOND DARKNESS

Friday Evening.

As the twilight fades into early darkness, Bill and Martha relax in the quiet aftermath of a very difficult and trying day. Suddenly Mary exclaims, "I'm worried! Bill! I'm Scared!" Bill, picking up on Mary's sense of alarm, is about to speak when Mary continues, "I just can't see how we're going to get through the winter. Money's very tight right now, but it's more than that Bill. There's just not enough money anymore to meet basic needs; we're barely keeping up with food, rent, and taxes. Since the Republicans abandoned Social Security and Medicare, most of what little income we bring in goes to medical expenses.

"I do appreciate how you feel" Martha, "we lost our pensions to the plant closure in the "Hedge Fund" hostile takeover debacle, and the money that came from the forced sale of the house due to rising property taxes just vanished in last year's speculation financial collapse."

After a long pause, Bill says, "You know, Martha, we're 70 years old, worked hard all our lives to raise three children, and sacrificed to remain debt free. Yet we find ourselves struggling to survive in our last days. And we're not alone; most of the young families in the neighborhood with only part-time low-wage work available are in the same situation. However, there is some good news: the election is next month."

"Now - That - Is - Just - Great!" Martha responds with a sigh, "The Republicans have promised economic growth, more jobs, and prosperity "even for the poor" for decades, and all that's left for most of us is subsistence living, increasing debt, and tax cuts for the wealthy.

Martha, looking at Bill with some hesitation, continues, "Now that I think of it, I heard that Republican "Grim Reaper" on cable news the other night comment - people like us 'should have thought of tomorrow's needs before we had children.'

"I know," Bill laments, "I understand all too well, Martha. We are in every sense a people politically betrayed, abandoned, and forgotten. And here we are, Martha, just "surplus people" existing in a Conservative "Trickle-Down" swamp of injustice, corruption, and greed"

II

The inference of betrayal of the "general welfare" of a People of Liberty which Galbraith makes reference still begs the question: How should we a People of Liberty, who swear allegiance to protect the Constitution of the United States against all "enemies" foreign and domestic, view an American "special interest" political-economic takeover of America's democratic institutions and the livelihood of the American people?

The Constitution is cogently clear the "national interest" of the nation is the "general welfare" of the people. Do we not as a nation consider a "foreign" adversary as any person, nation, or ideology with an intent or action to harm the "national interest" and the American way of life? More to the point, when we ask ourselves, "who do we say we are," do we ever consider the essence of "who we are" as a People of Liberty is life itself in the presence of a just and economically stable functional democracy? Do we see in ourselves the Founder's core meaning of the "Declaration of Independence" as the embodiment every person's "inalienable right to life"? Do we feel in our everyday Conservative "trickle-down" world of "every man for himself" the assurance of democracy of every person's "inalienable right to life" comes down you and me, our children, and our posterity?

It is for a People of Liberty in this American moment to behold this *"country belongs to the people,"* and the right every Citizen of Democracy in this political moment to exercise "the power and the duty" of the people "to protect themselves and their own welfare."

> **RETURN** Constitutional preeminence to America's representational democratic governance;
>
> **RESTORE** the protection of the "general welfare" as the primary imperative of the "national Interest;"
>
> **RENEW** America's founding "life" imperative of every person's "Inalienable Right to Life," equal access to a secure living-wage job, healthcare, and education;, and "equal justice before the law";
>
> **REVOKE** America's vested interest electoral financial dominance for public funded campaign financing and legislated mandated uninhibited universal voting.

Clearly every suffering American living poor in desperation and despair understands the political reality of today's "big money" dominated predatory culture of Profit over People is not the democratic America of Washington, Jefferson, and Lincoln. The political and economic "financial bondage" of the Conservative

Lives for Profit Subsistence Trickle-Down Society is nothing less than the return of the "let them eat cake" culture of divine right governance. The Republican brutal everyday culture of mercantile greed now dominates the life of every citizen and impoverished family struggling to survive the tragic human suffering, misery, and despair of the Republican "trickle-down" economic agenda. It now falls to the people as Lord Acton reminds us, "… *to make up for the want of legal responsibility … for absolute power corrupts absolutely*".

Today the ***"CALL OF LIBERTY"*** *beckons* a free democratic People, conceived in *"Liberty, Equality, and Justice,"* to a *Great Patriotic Renewal* of *Integrity, Trust, and Truth* to a Democratic America politically FREE of "big money" political-economic dominance and a *Rebirth of American Democracy that RESTORES*

> ***"To the People" a Representative***
> ***Democratic Republic "Of the People"***
> ***dedicated to the rule of law, equal***
> ***opportunity, and the Constitutional***
> ***rights of citizenship to "Life, Liberty, and***
> ***the "Pursuit of Happiness" for***
> ***"Ourselves and Our Posterity."***

The political-economic suffering of today's Republican predatory *"survival of the fittest"* culture of individual extremism and concentrated wealth brings to mind echoes of yesterday's freedom that cry out for a People of Liberty United in Freedom to VOTE the return to an American democracy "of, by, and for" the people. Some points to consider in the restoration of a people's Constitutional Democratic America of "Freedom, Equality, and Justice for All" would include the following:

ABOLISH "Corporate Personhood.

CONTROL GLOBAL WARMING through a measured public policy mandated transformation of America's fossil fuel dependency to a 21st Century American Renewable Clean Energy Infrastructure.

DECREE a *mandated living-wage income*, affordable national healthcare and education, government insured portable pension retirement security, and broad consumer product safety and environmental protections;

DEMILITARIZE the law enforcement culture of punitive extremism;

END private Prisons for Profit and all outsourced privatized government services;

ENFORCE the *Sherman Antitrust Act* and regulatory control over acquisitions and Mergers;

ENSURE everyone contributes a fair share to the national income - citizens, non-citizens, and all forms business profitability;

IMPOSE *regulatory controls* and tax liability on Hedge Fund and Private Equity operations;

LEGISLATE binding procedural mandates and real-time oversight accountability measures regardless of the political party in power that will ensure the function of America's Constitutional three co-equal branches of government;

LEVY a *transaction tax on monetary instruments bought and sold;*

MANDATE American *ownership of domestic media* networks that impact the national interest and truth oversight accountability;

MODERENIZE the *national the infrastructure* with a comprehensive publicl funded National Infrastructure Public Works Program;

PROHIBIT *"dark money"* campaign financing, voter suppression, political district gerrymandering;

REAFFIRM America's *inalienable to the right to life* as a right of citizenship for all generations;

REFORM America's electoral political process to (1) guarantee the voting rights of every American citizen absent party/state interference, (2) legislate public funded campaign financing, and (3) abolish the Electoral College;

REINSTATE *deregulated controls and protections* oversight accountability to commercial investment institutions;

RESTORE *parliamentary principles* of legislative procedure enforcing a fair representation of the people's general welfare and will of the electorate;

RETURN to the economic principles of a well-regulated *competitive fair market economy;*

REVIVE the "rule of law, equal justice under the law, and oversight accountability for American finance, business, and politics;

STRENGTHEN America's *democratic institutions*, breakup of "too-big-to-fail" monopolies: big tech giants, broad-casting and media consortiums, and financial institutions and cartels.

III

As citizens of freedom and democracy struggling to endure the "Trickle-Down" reality of want, desperation, and despair in this *"survival of the fittest"* Republican moment, Supreme Court Justice Louis D. Brandeis warned that we must as a People of Liberty be informed and vigilant to the greed, perils, and injustice of wealth concentration in the hands of a few, emphasizing that

> ***"We may have democracy***
> ***or we may have***
> ***concentrated wealth***
> ***in the hands of a few,***
> ***but we can't have both."***

The concentration and control of America's wealth "in the hands of a few" politically assured by an entrenched Republican power base are the defining focus of the Conservative "trickle-down" predatory "survival of the fittest" political agenda. For no other reason this is the economic predatory objective of the "big money" political takeover of America and its institutions, and the inability of America's workers to secure productive living-wage employment. The Republican political demise of yesterday's America is in this American moment the Republican legislated "trickle-down" predatory Lives for Profit "survival of the fittest" world of *"you're on your own" America.*

The Founding mechanism of Constitutional "checks and balances" of co-equal branches of government was designed specifically to prevent the exercise of authoritarian power and the concentration of wealth in the hands of a privileged plutocracy. The Forty-Year Republican takeover of America's political and economic institutions is for every suffering American today the struggle to survive the Conservative political-economic oppression of the Republican predatory "trickle-down" subsistence economy. The question before us fundamental to the future of American democracy in an America of "Liberty and Justice for All" is uncomplicated and straightforward: Are we a People of Liberty willing to electorally confront America's Republican ideological "survivalist" political reality of fascist greed, poverty, and desperation?

Yesterday's free democratic America is today's free democratic people infused as in days gone by with Liberty's most cherished values of Freedom. Is it for us, the electorate of America, to redress the American tragedy of Conservative predatory "Trickle-Down" poverty and desperation of this American moment, and return America to a Constitutional democracy of living-wage jobs, universal lifesaving healthcare, affordable education and housing, and for all Americans a long hard-earned dignified retirement.

For decades the Republican political dominance over America's democracy and its political institutions has abrogated the Constitutional obligations of the state to the Conservative "big money" power establishment of "individual" freedom "without a network of obligations" to pillage and plunder at will whatever the collateral damage to any individual, community, or the nation.

In societies historically akin to an ideological "Social Darwin" "Trickle-Down" world in times past, history suggests that citizenship in such a New Political Order of "individual extremism" is inevitably tied to political reliability and restraint, and economic viability. And, the politically designated "unworthy" who consume the valuable resources of the state will be subject to some form of state sanction. Is this the coming final "Trickle-Down" ideological reality of a new age of American "individual extremism"? Is this advanced Conservative Social Darwin Society to be a *"survival of the world"* of Euthanasia Care Centers for the terminally ill and Forced Labor Camps for the "unworthy" designated "surplus people" od America struggling day by day struggling to survive as politically designated "vermin," freeloaders" and "parasites,": America's vulnerable, the destitute, the disabled, the elderly retired living in poverty, and the chronically unemployed?

Is this not the time for every citizen to examine how we see ourselves as a Constitutional people whose Founder Fathers endeavored to guarantee that the *"nation exists to serve its citizens" and the function of responsible government is to promote and protect the "general welfare" of the people?*

Yesterday's competitive free market capitalism based on supply and demand died in the 1980 election of the Republican "Trickle-Down Supply Side" Revolution and the subsequent Republican legislated predatory "Trickle-Down" Profit over People subsistence casino America. Today's America of income inequality, poverty, hunger, and homelessness is the realization of the Republican legislated transformation of an American democracy that once embraced the security and welfare of the American family as the cornerstone of the nation.

In a democracy "OF, BY, and FOR" the People, it is the functional imperative of government to provide the means necessary for every citizen to be able to earn a respectable living-wage and live a dignified quality of life in economic security, peace, and justice. The resolution to today's "crisis in democracy" is nothing less than a return to a prosperous America for the many NOT just the few. It is for us, the people of America in this American moment, to protect "the general welfare" in a democratic America "of the people" that will deliver to America's People of Liberty the civil liberties, economic security, and Justice under the law through:

Protected universal voting rights,
Regulated market economy,
Secure living-wage jobs,
Affordable housing and education,
Government-backed retirement security,
and
National life-saving healthcare
As a democratic right of
Every citizen's "inalienable right to life.

IV

I often wonder in these difficult times how a democratic people relate to the reality of truth in a corrupt predatory world of "alternative facts". Truth, of course, is what it always has been, the reality of what is supported by personal observation or reliable documented facts. For most Americans I still see truth in this political era of Republican alternative reality the armor that protects a democratic people from the political lies, deceit, and subterfuge that seeks to hide "the reality of what is" hidden in the shadows of greed, corruption, and injustice.

Now as I bring to a close this narrative of yesterday's America of Liberty and Justice, and today's quest for Freedom and Hope, I again struggle with thoughts of yesterday's prosperous America of "what once was," and the political-economic reality of today's America of pretense, lies, and "alternate facts" that for over four decades of Republican predatory "Trickle-Down" dominance has reduced the People of America to an impoverished "surplus people" held captive in a Conservative *survival of the fittest* existence of want and desperation.

I see that America once prosperous, stable, and secure, an America at economic peace when the reality of the America Dream was limited only to one's desire, will, and courage to make it happen. I see a time when America was the Beacon of Liberty, when everyone had access to a productive living-wage employment, affordable healthcare, housing, and education, and the promise of a retirement with dignity in old age. I see an America that was for a People of Liberty the Golden Age of the American experience; a time we celebrated as a free democratic people a shared belief in an America of "one Nation under God."

The America of personal liberty and income prosperity that once was but a generation ago is gone - dead, dismantled and discarded – stolen from a trusting democratic People of Liberty through decades of political betrayal in the name of fairy-tale profits, wealth concentration, and the elimination of middle class America that today has left the American people shattered and impoverished in a Republican Predatory "Trickle-Down" Subsistence Society of want, and desperation

The Republican 1971 Powell agenda for the political-economic takeover of America set in motion in 1981 is today the Conservative "Trickle-Down" America of this "2023" moment. The 1981 Republican "Trickle-Down" Revolution "white supremacy" objectives of achieving absolute power, concentrating America's wealth in the hands of a few, and seizing economic dominance over the people of America is the reality for every American struggling in today's Republican predatory "Trickle-Down" subsistence America of the *"survival of the fittest."*

Conservative "Trickle-Down" prosperity was sold in 1980 as the Republican life-saving program that would resolve the economic downturn of the 1970s, create higher paying jobs, and extend prosperity to everyone. The political reality, of course, is that the Republican political establishment transformed America over four decades of political deception and deceit into a nation of polarization, and legislated into law through political manipulation and disinformation an America of "surplus" people *"responsible for their own fate."*

The consequences of this four-decade Republican "Trickle-Down" campaign of political oppression, is that we are a disenfranchised democratic people who daily bear witness to ugly Republican legislative autocratic governance, institutional paralysis, political corruption, and the overt political emasculation of justice.

This is *the "you're on your own"* Conservative "Trickle-Down" world of Republican legislated *"individual extremism"* of *the "survival of the fittest."* At its crux, it is the Conservative orchestrated political-economic world that the people of America struggle daily to make ends meet with a subsistence existence of temporary work, poverty wages, and a lifetime of chronic debt.

V

We see across the nation an America politically and economically bankrupt, a country on the verge of economic collapse at any given moment for the sole benefit of enriching the financial elite. And, tragically, only a few are given to acknowledge the real elephant in the room for what it is: the "big money" vested interest politicized predatory ideological world of *"political economy"* in the name of business efficiency, maximum profitability, and monopoly dominance that decrees the people of America are *"responsible for their own fate,"* the Republican "Trickle-Down" ideological mantra every citizen has the freedom to "fend for yourself," to "become surplus," and exercise your "freedom to starve" in a Conservative financialized subsistence-wage debt-based predatory economy.

The American Citizen in today's Republican "Trickle-Down" predatory world is a non-person, just a disposable pawn, mercantile fodder in a Conservative world of Creators, Producers, Sustainers, and Parasites used to maximize short-term profits oblivious to any regard for the "general welfare" of the people or America's commercial and economic national interests.

Keep in mind in this electoral moment of lost jobs, national hunger, and human desperation, the core political reality of the Conservative Social Darwin ideological imperative of "political economy" is upfront *the more surplus workers, the more profitable our operations."* And for everybody else - well, it's just the same old Conservative predatory "Trickle-Down" reality of your everyday *"survival of the fittest"* America of organized systemic exploitation, struggle, and despair.

The Founding Fathers would be appalled to witness the moral transformation and political descent of America into what is today's Republican predatory impoverished "Trickle-Down" America of national greed, concentrated wealth, greed and corruption, and political hypocrisy.

George Washington in his 1796 Farewell Address called for the preservation of religion and morality as the abiding foundation of the nation. Washington stressed that ***of all the dispositions and habits which lead to political prosperity, religion and morality are indispensable supports. In vain would that man claim the tribute of patriotism, who should labor to subvert these great pillars of human happiness…these firmest props of the duties of men and citizens, the mere politician…ought to respect and to cherish…"***

Thomas Jefferson asserted in the "Declaration of Independence" ratified by the Congress on July 4, 1776: ***We hold these truths to be self-evident, that all men are created equal, that they are endowed by their Creator with certain***

inalienable rights, that among these are life, liberty, and the pursuit of happiness!"

James Madison, Father of the Constitution, believed in the dignity and equality of every person and through the Bill of Rights sought to protect the security and opportunity of every America to live life to the fullest, writing: *"We have staked the whole future of American civilization, not upon the power of government, far from it. We've staked the future of all our political institutions upon our capacity ... to sustain ourselves according to the Ten Commandments of God."*

John Adams, 2nd President of the United States, wrote: *"the general principle of which the fathers achieved independence were...the general principles of Christianity... I then believed, and now believe that those general principles of Christianity are as eternal and immutable as the existence and attributes of God... Our constitution was made only for a moral and religious people... It is religion and morality alone which can establish the principles upon which freedom can securely stand."*

In more recent times, **Justice Earl Warren,** Justice of the Supreme Court Justice, in a 1954 interview published in Time Magazine (February 14, 1954), stated that he believed the *"entire Bill of Rights came into being because of the knowledge our forefathers had of the bible and belief in it...freedom of belief, of expression, of assembly, of petition, the dignity of*

the individual, the sanctity of the home, equal justice under the law..."

The truth hurts, we are told. Of course, the truth hurts. And the truth for today's America of Washington, Jefferson, and Madison is there's nothing more "liberating" than the feeling of "Freedom, Equality, and Justice" that can relieve the pain of injustice. For today's Republican "Trickle- Down" subsistence America the pain of injustice can only be remedied with productive living-wage jobs, affordable lifesaving healthcare for all, and retirement security in an America of "Liberty and Justice for All."

We are what we believe and the values we hold most sacred: freedom, family, truth, fairness, justice, concern for another's well being. We each have the "liberty" to do that which is good, just, and honest. It is these values "We the People" have asserted over the generations to make known to one and all what it means to be a citizen of America. To believe in an America of "Liberty, Equality, and Justice" is for every patriotic American to proclaim and honor through the democratic process the values that assure "Liberty and Justice for All".

Surely, **"PATRIOTISM"** is loyalty first to the Constitution, America's Founding values of Truth, Freedom, Democracy, and the Rule of Law" that defines who we are as a free democratic People of Liberty.

Now, as we debate our children's political world of tomorrow, the political imperative of this American moment is for each of us to keep upper most in our political consciousness the reality,

EVERY VOTE MATTERS

FOR
FREEDOM AND DEMOCRACY
EVERY VOTE MATTERS!

FOR
LIVING WAGE JOBS
EVERY VOTE MATTERS!

FOR
LIFESAVING HEALTHCARE
EVERTY VOTE MATTERS!

FOR
JUSTICE BEFORE THE LAW
EVERY VOTE MATTERS!

FOR
LIBERTY, TRUTH, JUSTICE
EVERY VOTE MATTERS!

TO BE FREE AMERICA
EVERY VOTE MATTERS!

TEN
FREE TO CHOOSE

Henry Wallace

ON
AMERICAN FASCISM

The method of American fascism *"is to poison the channels of public information. With a fascist the problem is never how best to present the truth to the public but how best to use the news to deceive the public into giving the fascist and his group more money or more power.*

The American fascist claims *"to be super patriots, but they would destroy every liberty guaranteed by the constitution.*

The America fascist *"demands free enterprise but they are spokesmen for monopoly and vested interests.*

The American fascist's *"final objective is directed to the capture of political power so that, using the power of the state and the power*

> **of the market simultaneously, they may keep
> the common man in eternal subjugation."**

The triumphant Republican 40-year campaign to rescue "capitalism from democracy, "financially subjugate the people of America, and lay the foundation for the political takeover of democracy is the Republican America of this American moment. In a generation, America has been "turned upside down" into a Republican ideological state of individual extremism of the "survival of the fittest," a predatory - deregulated - debt-based America of power supremacy and human bondage. Today's political reality is that the wealth of the nation concentrated in the hands of a few has been used to attack the very foundational notion of government "by and for" the people.

January 6, 2021, make no mistake, was America's "Rubicon" moment. For every American in today's electoral moment "the die is cast." It is either DEMOCRACY OR AUTOCRACY for America's tomorrows.

The strength of who we are as a People of Liberty *"is seen in the things we stand for,"* Theodore Roosevelt reminded us. While the political-economic reality of America before us since the advent of the 1981 Republican "Trickle-Down" Revolution is but a Conservative predatory "survival of the fittest" world of vulture capitalism, lawless exploitation, and suppression of basic civil liberties, the things we stand for as a People of Liberty have not changed: Constitutional Democracy, the rule of law, secure living wage jobs, and the "inalienable right to life, liberty, and the pursuit of happiness." This is the idea of America; this is our founding birthright; this is who we are as a People of Liberty. The hold of political "individual extremism" manifested in today's Republican ideological world of the "survival of the fittest" is the reality of the Conservative Culture of Death shrouded in a web of lies that blind, deafen, and deceive.

The destructive "evil" of "designing men" of wealth and power reigns over the Betrayal of America in this electoral moment. The reality of authoritarian despotism has to date permitted the Republican ideology of political "extremism" to tear down the ability of the American people to purse the blessings of "life, liberty, and pursuit of happiness."

As a People of Liberty in 2024 remember,

> The **REPUBLICAN** financialized debt-based subsistence-wage, casino "Trickle-Down" economy;

> The **REPUBLICAN** state racially oriented voter rights suppression laws disenfranchising tens of millions of voters;

> The **REPUBLICAN** state voter nullification laws overruling the "will of the people;"

> The **REPUBLICAN** "rigged" gerrymandering of state voter districts in pursuit of Conservative white power supremacy;

> The **REPUBLICAN** state pandemic anti-vaccine political initiatives that unnecessarily caused tens of thousands of "unvaccinated Covid deaths;

> The **REPUBLICAN** "Climate Change Denial" legislative obstruction in the name of "Profit over People" destroying our children's world of tomorrow;

> The **REPUBLICAN** legislative "obstruction" politics blocking today's "democratic" human

infrastructure for lifting working families out of poverty and the "Trickle-Down" human bondage of profit supremacy.

Regardless the Republican Party's presidential nominee, the Republican promised agenda for 2024 America is the Conservative Fifty-Year strategy for a protracted Republican transformation of American democracy through,

DISMANTLING America's political and state institutions;

POLITIZING the government career "civil serve;"

DEREGULATION of the "rule of law" into a politically acceptable state of "lawlessness" in politics, business, finance, and government;

TAX CUTS for the ultra-rich and corporations;

PRIVATIZATION of Social Security, Medicare, and the medical Affordable Care Act; and, most importantly,

POLITICAL SUBVERSION of norms, intensifying ethnic and cultural division, and inciting violence to radicalize supporters;

DISINFORMATION poisoning of the public discourse; and

SEIZURE of absolute power by any means.

The Republican campaign agenda for 2024 is the political promise to literally restructure American Democracy into a "maga" 1930s racist authoritarian model of "fascism."

Four decades of Republican political economic and social engineering for the concentration of wealth and power of America presents the electorate with a compromised America on the fringe of forever losing the cherished freedoms of democracy, and a Constitutional America dedicated to the rule of law, equal opportunity, and the common good. *"The spirit of resistance to government is so valuable on certain occasions,"* wrote Thomas Jefferson in a letter to Abigail Adams in 1787, *"that I wish it always to be kept alive."* That "certain occasion" for today's besieged democratic America is so blatantly and visibly present in the perverse human suffering that pervades the people of America

America's 2024 electoral moment is America's electoral grand finale of the Conservative 40-year REPUBLICAN ASSAULT ON DEMOCRACY and political Betrayal of the American People. Today's Conservative "Trickle-Down" reality of want, desperation, and despair and the concentration of America's wealth and power in the hands of "designing men" is the Republican 2024 "Trickle-Down" promise for tomorrow's America. Consider we must as a People of Liberty the future of America as we reflect on where we stand as a suffering democratic people of "liberty" after 40 years of Republican political betrayal:

First, reflect on the present reality of President Franklin D. Roosevelt's warning that "fascism" would come to America in the form of profit supremacy and monopoly dominance, if *"the people tolerate the growth of private power to a point where it becomes stronger than their democratic state … That is fascism … ownership of government … by a group or controlling private power… Democracy is not safe if its business system does not provide employment … in such a way as to sustain an acceptable standard of living"* for its people.

Secondly, consider that following the 1971 Powell declaration of "war against democracy" and the American middle class, the Republican political establishment set out to reconstruct America, the criminal justice system, and the electoral system in favor of the wealthy power elite. Through deregulation, privatization, wealthy tax cuts, and voter restrictions, American democracy is today a nation of wealth and power concentrated in the 1%, a "financialized casino" of laissez-faire profiteers, an economy of monopolized production, distribution, and trade, and, for the people, a debt-based existence of service jobs, subsistence wages, and retirement poverty on the streets of America.

Thirdly, understand that America's democracy of this American moment is in the hands of today's Conservatives that have relentlessly sought to marginalize democracy, morality, and truth, usurp the power of the state, and, through the power of "dark money," reconfigure America's Republican state legislatures to ensure forever a Conservative hold on political power. Today we must remind ourselves as Dietrich Bonheoffer warned "***TO SEE EVIL AND NOT CALL IT EVIL IS EVIL; NOT TO SPEAK IS TO SPEAK; NOT TO ACT IS TO ACT.***"

The political-economic reality of America is everywhere evident across a suffering America where the Conservative ideological extremism of unhampered capital supremacy of the "survival of the fittest" reigns supreme over the lives of an abandoned surplus people and the demise of American democracy.

With the Republican obstruction of the National Voting Rights Act, the Republican political establishment has laid the groundwork to achieve the "fascist" authoritarianism of absolute power supremacy. America's democratic heritage, traditions, and institutions have been successfully eroded for the Conservative elimination of democracy itself in America. Given a Republican takeover of Congress in 2022, the Republican political "assault on democracy" envisioned in the "Powell Memorandum" of 1971 to save "capitalism from democracy" will forever hold America's free democratic people in the human bondage of want, desperation, and despair."

Across America, from the Atlantic to the Pacific, from the mountains and prairies to the desert wastelands, in the cities, and in the towns and villages, America's Great democracy is under siege. Notes former Republican Max Boot, author *of The Corrosion of Conservatism: Why I Left the Right* (2018), *"I have no faith that we will remain a democracy if Republicans win power."*

The political reality of 2024 is America's survival moment of democracy that will determine forever whether the promise of Freedom, Equality, and Justice in America is to survive into a "new age" of Constitutional governance "of the people, by the people, and for the people" of America.

In 2020, the people of America voted to renew Martin Luther King's dream of an equal America, an America that values the "inalienable right to life" over wealth creation, an America whose birthright of "*liberty and justice for all*" calls each of us today to undo the burden of political "dark money" tyranny, break the bonds of greed, corruption, and injustice, and ensure a decent standard of living for every American.

The *"spirit of resistance"* called for by Thomas Jefferson in times of tyrannical national peril demands that "We the People" in 2024 come together to "constitutionally" resolve the Republican corruption of democracy.

The Election of 2024 is the "last battle" in the coming final struggle for DEMOCRACY in America. For the people of America in this apocalyptic electoral moment, as Edmund Burke so gravely observed, *"THE ONLY THING FOR EVIL TO TRIUMPH IS FOR GOOD PEOPLE TO DO NOTHING."*

"You cannot escape the responsibility of tomorrow,"* warned Abraham Lincoln, *"by evading it today." Tomorrow's political reality of Freedom and Democracy in America is in our hands. The choice for every citizen in 2024 is very straight forward as historian Matt Stoller forewarned in 2019: that we vote to knowingly allow *"a small aristocracy governing…to serve concentrated power, or free ourselves from concentrated power."*

***The Hour has Come; The Moment is Here; the Time is Now for the return of Democracy, Truth, and Justice to an America* "Of the People, By the People, For the People."**

2024 may very well be America's "one time" opportunity for a free democratic people to **EMBRACE** the "truth" of an America "In God We Trust;" **RETURN** of the "rule of law" to business, finance, and politics; and **RESTORE** America's founding vision of government *"by the people for the people"* that will ***"insure** domestic Tranquility…**establish** Justice…**promote** the general Welfare…and **secure** the Blessings of Liberty…for ourselves and our posterity."*

We the People
It is for every citizen to pick up
the Torch of Liberty and
"Bring Light Into the Darkness"
for One America of
Liberty, Truth, and Justice

FREEDOM CALLING

I HEAR
The toll of
LIBERTY'S BELL
Ringing a great
PATRIOTIC RENEWAL

I HEAR the sound
Of distant drums
Echoing Freedom's Call
For LIBERTY, TRUTH,
AND JUSTICE

I HEAR above
The din of battle for
The Soul of America
Cry out for a
FREE AMERICA

I HEAR the
Sound of Liberty
Beckoning a proud
Democratic people to the
LIGHT OF A NEW DAWN

EPILOGUE

With
**PRESIDENT
THEODORE ROOSEVELT**

ON

AMERICAN DEMOCRACY

*"The people have the right, the power,
and the duty to protect themselves and
their own welfare."*

"I believe in pure democracy. With Lincoln, I hold this country, with its institutions, belongs to the people who inhabit it. Whenever they shall grow weary of the existing government, they can exercise their Constitutional right of amending it.

"We Progressives believe that the people have the right, the power, and the duty to protect themselves and their own welfare; that human rights are supreme over all other rights; that wealth should be the servant, not the master, of the people.

"We believe that unless representative government does absolutely represent the people it is not representative government at all. We test the worth of all men and all measures by asking how they contribute to the welfare of the men, women, and children of whom this nation is composed.

"We are engaged in one of the great battles of the age-long contest waged against privilege on behalf of the common welfare. We hold it a prime duty of the people to free our government from the control of money in politics. For this purpose we advocate, not as ends of themselves but as weapons

119

in the hands of the people, all government devices which will make the representatives of the people more easily and certainly responsible to the will of the people.

"This country, as Lincoln said, belongs to the people. So do the natural resources which make it rich. They supply the basis of our prosperity now and hereafter. In preserving them, which is a national duty, we must not forget that monopoly is based on the control of national resources ... and that it will help the people little to conserve our natural wealth of concentrated power and the benefits which it can yield are secured to the people. Let us remember, also ... that the principle of making the best of all have requires with equal or greater insistence that we shall stop the waste of human life in industry, and prevent the waste of human welfare which flows from the unfair use of concentrated power and wealth in the hands of men whose eagerness for profit blinds them to the cost of what they do.

"I am emphatically a believer in constitutionalism, and because of this fact I know less emphatically protest against any theory that would make the constitution a means of thwarting instead of securing the absolute right of the people to rule themselves and to provide for their own social and industrial well-being. All constitutions – those of the states no less than that of the nation – are designed and must be interpreted and administered so as to fit human rights.

"The power is the people's, and only the people ... It is a false constitutionalism ... to endeavor by the exercise of a perverted ingenuity to seem to give to the people full power and at the same time trick them out of it. Yet this precisely what is done in every case ... where the servants of the people set themselves up to be the masters of the people ... The power of the people to enact the law should not be subject to debate. To hold the contrary view is to be false to the cause of the people, to the cause of American democracy.

"We should discriminate between two purposes we have in view. The first is the effort to provide what are themselves the ends of good government; the second is the effort to provide proper machinery for the advancement of these ends. The ends of good government in our democracy are to secure by genuine popular rule a high average of moral and material well-being among our citizens ... The only prosperity worth having is that which affects the mass of the people ... I hold it our duty to see that the wage worker, the small producer, the ordinary consumer, shall get their fair share of the benefit of business prosperity.

"Now ... It is imperative to exercise over big business ... control and supervision ... All business must be conducted under the law, and all business men, big or small, must act justly. But a wicked big interest is necessarily more dangerous to the community than a wicked little interest. Big business in the past has been responsible for much of the special privilege which must be sparingly cut out of our national life.

"Government regulation of big business is ... needed ... Among the states that have entered this field Wisconsin has taken a leading place ... They have initiated the kind of progressive government which means not merely the preservation of true democracy but the extension of the principle of true democracy into industrialism as well as politics.

"This is precisely the attitude we should take towards big business. It is the practical application of the principle of the square deal ... In other words, our demand is that big business give the people a square deal and the people give a square deal to any man engaged in big business who honestly endeavors to do what is right and proper. All business into which the element of monopoly in any way or degree ... should be carefully supervised, regulated, and controlled by government authority...[if not] broken up.

"But we should not fear, if necessary, to bring the regulation of big [business] to the point of controlling conditions so that the wage worker shall have a wage more than sufficient to cover the bare cost of living, and hours of work not so excessive as to wreck his strength by the strain of unending toil and leave him unfit to do his duty as a good citizen on the community.

"Whatever the practices upon the past of large combinations may threaten to discourage such a man or to deny to him that which in the judgment of the community is a square deal should be specifically defined by the statutes as crimes. And in every case the individual ... responsible for such unfair dealing should be punished.

"But we should so shape conditions that a fortune shall be obtained only in honorable fashion, in such fashion ... We stand for the rights of property, but we stand even more for the rights of man. We will protect the rights of the wealthy man, but we maintain that he holds his wealth subject to the community to regulate its business use as the public welfare requires."

Theodore Roosevelt,
Exposition of American democracy
before the Ohio State Constitutional
Convention in 1912,

WE ARE THE 99%

FREEDOM RISING

TODAY
"We"
REJOICE
In America's
HERITAGE
Of the
PEOPLE'S
INALIENABLE
RIGHT TO LIFE

TODAY
"We"
PROCLAIM
THIS LAND IS OUR LAND
"In God We Trust"
A NATION
Of
FREEDOM, EQUALITY,
AND JUSTICE

TODAY
The
SPIRIT OF AMERICA
RISES
Out of the Darkness
To CHAMPION A
PEOPLE OF LIBERTY
And an America
FOREVER FREE

FOREVER FREE?

"Are we dead? Orwell asks."
Shall we meet in the place
where there is no darkness?"

Up for grabs in 2024 is America's democracy and the founding vision of an America built on a *"bulwark against government… tyranny over the minds of the people… [and] in the fullness of time… freedom… equality…[and] justice"* for all the people.

With the 2024 election, as with the January 6, 2021 "maga" insurrection, we will again see is a political reality few don't want to see, or perhaps, just don't want to believe can happen in America. Here we see again as Chris Hedges writes *in America Fascists,* The seditionists "arrayed against democracy, *"are waiting to strike, [seeking an opportunity] that will allow them to shred the Constitution… This movement is bent on our destruction… [They] hate the liberal, enlightened world formed by the Constitution… They have one goal — its destruction."*

And again in 2024, the Man on the White Horse cometh as in 2016 to take advantage of a political crisis, social turmoil, and economic downturns to take control of the democratic state and create an America of "fascist" political corruption, chaos, and destruction.

Given a Republican controlled "House of "burn or rule' politics and the political extremism of Republican lies and false narratives, we can expect the coming election to be exposed to every Conservative political resource of political radicalism. The Conservative "maga" establishment can be expected make every effort in a grand finale "Assault on Democracy" to seize absolute political power in 2024.

Now as we approach the Conservative "apocalyptic" reality of 2024, we must appreciate that 2024 is not just another election. This is the electoral moment where the future of Democracy, Freedom, and Justice in America is on the ballot. Every ballot cast in 2024, is a ballot for one issue, and one issue only: **"POWER!" - the "power" to preserve or destroy "democracy in America for tomorrow's America and future generations to come.**

For a reminder of what a Republican power grab in 2024 would bring to America, imagine for a moment the tyranny and horror of Republican authoritarian rule over a "lawless" racist America of anger, hate, and chaos, unfettered predatory capitalism, and the terror of unbridled gun violence on the streets of America

Presently, the 2024 Republican Orwellian "maga" frontrunner, a twice impeached, four-time criminally indicted insurrectionist, is being unequivocally candid in laying out the Republican "maga" political supremacy agenda for restructuring American democracy into a corrupt political authoritarian order. Simply stated: **the Republican agenda for a 2025 America on a Republican "maga" assumption of power is a 1930s racist authoritarian model of "fascism."**

The moment is now we come together as a free democratic people for an America of secure democratic institutions, a strong middle class, stable living-wage jobs, and a prosperous America of Liberty, Truth, and Justice - an America for all the people "free" of the greed, corruption, and injustices of today's Republican "laissez-faire" world of "Trickle-Down" debt-based casino "individual extremism of want, desperation, and despair

AMERICA AWAKE!

There stands
our once
Great Democracy
Today
Betrayed and Abandoned
Destitute In the Shambles
Of Want and Despair
Gone
Our Livelihood
Stability and Security
Our Cherished Freedoms
Now
Just Rampant Corruption
"Trickle-Down" Servitude
And Desperation for All

TRUTH MATTERS

HISTORY IS TRUTH

"Facts are stubborn things.
Facts are true things.
Facts are reliable.
They cannot be ignored.
History is truth teaching by
example. We may miss the
truth by perverting the history,
but truth is in the facts of
history."
E.M. Bounds

CARNIVAL OF SHAME
A REFERENCE GUIDE

ANDERSEN, Kurt, *Evil Geniuses: The Unmaking of America: A Recent History* NY: Random House, 2020)

ARNADE, Chris, *Dignity: Seeking Respect in Back Row America* (NY: Penguin Random House, 2019)

ABRAMSKY, Sasha, *The America Way of Poverty: How the Other Half Still Lives* (NY: Nation Books, 2013)

BATTISTONE, Alyssa, **"Everything to Lose: The Struggle To Save the Planet," The Nation** (June 3/10, 2019)

BARTLETT, Donald L. and James B. STEELE, *The Betrayal of the American Dream* (NY: Public Affairs, 2012)

BELZER, David and David Wayne, *Corporate Conspiracies: How Wall Street Took Over Washington* (NY: Skyhorse Publishing, 2017)

BENEN, Steve, *The Imposters: How the Republicans Quit Governing and Seized American Politics* (NY: HarperCollins Publishers, 2020)

BRILL, Steve, **Tailspin:** *The People and Forces behind America's Fifty-Year Fall – and Those Fighting to Reverse It* (NY: Alfred A. Knoph, 2018)

BURLEIGH, Nina, *"The Making of Dark Money King," The New Republic* (June 2023)

CAPPINS, McKay, **"Newt Gingrich Says You're Welcome,"** *Atlantic* (November 2018)

CHAYES, Sarah, *On Corruption in America: And What Is at Stake* (NY: Alfred A. Knoph,2020)

COHEN, Adam, Supreme Inequality*: The Supreme Court's Fifty-Year Battle for a More Unjust America* (NY: Penguin Books, 2020)

CRIER, Catherine, **Patriot Acts:** *What Americans Must Do To Save the Republic* (NY: Threshold Editions, 2011)

COCKBURN, Andrew, *The Spoils of War: Power, Profit and the American War Machine* (NY: Verso Books, 2021)

CHURCHILL, Ward, *A Little Matter of Genocide: Holocaust and Denial in the Americas 1492 to the Present* (SF: City Lights Books, 1997)

COVERT, Bryce, **"Everyone Must Go: Hedge-Fund Owners Drive Sears and Toys "R" Us into Bankruptcy and Put Thousands of People Out of Work,"** *The Nation* (May 6, 2019)

DERBER, Charles and Yale MAGRASS**,** *The Surplus American: How the 1% Is Making Us Redundant* (Boulder, CO: Paradigm Publishers, 2012)

ELDERMAN, Peter, *Not A Crime Be Poor: The Criminalization of Poverty in America* (NY: The New Press, 2017)

ELLIS, Joseph J., **American Dialogue:** *The Founders And Us* (NY: Alfred A. Knoph, 2018)

FORNIER, Joseph R. I, ed., *The Language of Liberty: The Political Speeches and Writings of Abraham Lincoln* (Washington, D.C.: Regnery Publishing, Inc., 2009)

FRANKS, Thomas, *The Wrecking Crew: How Conservatives Ruined Government, Enriched Themselves, and Beggared the Nation* (NY: Holt Paperbacks, 2008)

GATES, Henry Louis, *Stony the Road: Reconstruction, White Supremacy, and the Rise of Jim Crow* (NY: Penguin Press, 2019)

GIBNEY, Bruce Cannon, *A Generation of Sociopaths: How the Baby Boomer Betrayed America* (NY: Hachette Books, 2017)

GIGANTES, Philippe*, Power and Greed: A Short History of the World (NY: Carrol & Graf Publishers, 2002)*

GLAUDE, Eddie S., Jr.*, Democracy in Black: How Race Still Enslaves the American Soul* (NY: Crown Publishers, 2016)

GREIDER, William M., *Who Will Tell the People: The Betrayal of American Democracy* (NY: Simon and Schuster, 1992)

GRUNDY, George W., *Death of a Nation: 9/11 and the Rise of Fascism in America* (NY: Skyhorse Publishing, 2017)

GUENDELSBERGER, Emily, *On the Clock: What Low-Wage Work Did to Me and How It Drives America Insane* (NY: Little, Brown and Company, 2019)

HARTMANN, Thom, *The Crash of 2016: The Plot to Destroy America* (NY: Twelve, 2014)

HARTMANN, Thom, *The Hidden History of Monopolies: How Big Business Destroyed the American Dream* (Oakland, CA: Berrett-Koehler Publishers, Inc, 2020)

HARTMANN, Thom, *The Hidden History of American Oligarchy: Reclaiming Our Democracy from the Ruling Class* (Oakland, CA: Berrett-Koehler Publishers, Inc, 2021)

HARTMANN, Thom, *Screwed: The Undeclared War Against the Middle Class* (San Francisco, CA 2006)

HEDGES, Chris, **American Fascists:** *The Christian Right and the War on America* (NY: Free Press, 2006)

HEDGES, Chris, *The World As It Is: Dispatches on the Myth of Human Progress* (NY: Nation Books, 2013)

HIGHTOWER, Jim, *Thieves in High Places: They've Stolen Our Country - And It's Time To Take It Back* (NY: Viking Penguin, 2003)

HONEY, Michael K., *To the Promised Land: Martin Luther King and the Fight for Economic Justice* (NY: W. W. Norton & Company, 2018)

HOBSON, John, *Imperialism: A Study* (London, 2011)

JONES, Matt wit Chris TOMLIN, *Mitch Please!: How Mitch McConnell Sold Out Kentucky (and America, Too),* (NY: Simon & Schuster, 2020)

KENDZIOR, Sarah, *Hiding in Plain Sight: The Invention of Donald Trump and the Erosion of America* (NY: Flatiron Book, 2020)

KARl, Jonathon, *Betrayal: The Final Act of the Trump Show* (NY: Penguin Random House LLC, 2022)

KLEINKNECHT, William, *The Man Who Sold the World: Ronald Reagan and the Betrayal of Main Street America* (NY: Nation Books, 2009)

LEFEBVRE, Georges, *The Coming of the French Revolution* (Princeton University Press, 1973)

LEHMANN, Chris, **"Lobbying for War,"** *The Nation* (November 27-December 4, 2023)

LOFGREN, Mike, *The Deep State: The Fall of the Constitution and the Rise of a Shadow Government* (NY: Viking Penguin, 2016)

LOFGREN, Mike, *The Party Is Over: How Republicans Went razy, Democrats Became Useless, and the Middle Class Got Shafted* (NY: Viking Penguin, 2012)

MACLEAN, Nancy, *Democracy in Chains: The Deep History of the Radical Right's Plan for America* (NY: Viking, 2017)

MAYER, Jane, *Dark Money: The Hidden History of the Billionaires Behind the Rise of the Radical Right* (NY: Doubleday, 2016)

McCULLOUGH, David, *The American Spirit: Who We Are and What We Stand For* (NY: Simon & Schuster 2017)

McGARITY, Thomas, *Freedom to Harm: The Lasting Legacy of the Laissez Faire Revival* (New Haven, Yale University Press, 2013)

MEACHAM, Jon, *The Soul of America: The Battle for Our Better Angels* (NY: Penguin Random House, 2018)

MILBANK, Dana, *The Destructionists: The Twenty-Five-Year Crack-Up of the Republican Party* (NY: Doubleday, 2022)

NATIONS, Scott, *A History of the United States in Five Crashes Stock Market Meltdowns That Defined A Nation* (NY: HarperCollins Publishers, 2017)

OLLER, John, *White Shoe: How a New Breed of Wall Street Lawyers Changed Big Business and the American Century* (NY: Penguin Random House, 2019)

PERLSTEIN, Rick, **"Prophets of Instability: How Finance Broke the Modern Corporations,"** *The Nation* (March 30, 2020)

PERLSTEIN, Rick, *Reaganland: America's Right Turn 1976-1980* (Simon & Schuster, 2020)

PETERS, Jeremy W., *Insurgency: How Republicans Lost Their Party and Got Everything They Ever Wanted* (NY: Crown, 2022)

Pilling, David, *The Delusion of Growth: Wealth, Poverty, and the Well-Being of Nations* (NY: Tim Duggan Books, 2018)

POWELL, Lewis F., Jr., *Memorandum:* **"Attack on the American Free Enterprise System," *August 23, 1971*,** Chamber of Commerce, Washington, D.C.

QUART, Alissa, *Squeezed: Why American Families Can't Afford America* (NY: HarperCollins, 2018)

RAMUS, Jack, *The Scourge of Neoliberalism: US Economic Policy from Reagan to Trump* (Atlanta, GA, Clarity Press, Inc., 2020)

RAMUS, Jack, *The War At Home: The Corporate Offensive from Ronald Reagan to George W. Bush* (San Ramon, CA: Kyklos Publicans, 2006)

REICH, Robert B., *Beyond Outrage: What Has Gone Wrong with Our Economy and Our Democracy, and How to Fix It* (NY: Vintage Books, 2012)

REICH, Robert B., *Saving Capitalism: For the Many, Not the Few* (NY: Alfred A. Knoph, 2015)

REICH, Robert B., *Supercapitalism: The Transformation of Business, Democracy, and Everyday Life* (NY: Alfred Knopf, 2007)

REID-HENRY, Simon, *Empire of Democracy: The Remaking of the West Since the Cold War, 1971-2017* (NY: Simon & Schuster, 2019)

RICHARDSON, Heather Cox, *"The Fight for our America," The New Republic* (November 2023)

RUSSELL, Dick, *Horsemen of the Apocalypse: The Men Who Are Destroying Life on Earth and What It Means for Our Children* (NY: Skyhorse Publishing, 2017)

SCHIFF, Adam, *Midnight in Washington: How We Almost Lost Our Democracy and Still Could* (NY: Random House, 2021)

SEIB, Gerald F., *We Should Have Seen It Coming: From Reagan to Trump – A Front-Row Seat to a Political Revolution* (NY: Random House, 2020)

SMITH Hedrick, *Who Stole the American Dream* (NY: Random House, 2012)

SHAXSON, Rick, *"Rural America Doesn't Have to Starve," The Nation* (March 30, 2020)

STERNBERG, Joseph C., *The Theft of a Decade: How the Baby Boomers Stole the Millennials' Econonic Future* (NY: PublicAffairs, 2019)

STIGLITZ, Joseph E*., People, Power, and Profits: Progressive Capitalism for an Age of Discontent* (NY: W. Norton & Company, 2019)

STOLLER, Matt, *Goliath: The 100-Year War between Monopoly Power and Democracy* (NY: Simon & chuster, 2019)

SULLIVAN, Teresa A., Elizabeth WARREN, and Jay Lawrence WESTROOK, *The Fragile Middle Class: Americans in Debt* (New Haven: Yale University Press, 2020)

TAYLOR, Miles, *Blowback: A Warning to Save Democracy from the Next Trump* (NY: Atria Books, 2023)

TIRADO, Linda, *Hand to Mouth: Living In Bootstrap America* (NY: Berkley Books, 2014)

TOMASKY, Michael, *"Donald Trump Against America,"* **The New Republic** (June 2023).

WALLACE, Vice President Henry**, Remarks on Fascism in America, New York Times**, April 9, 1944

WHITEHOUSE, Sheldon with Melanie Wachtell STINNETT, *Captured: The Corporate Infiltration of American Democracy* (NY: The New Press, 2017)

WINANT, Gabriel, **"No Going Back: The Power and Limits of the Anti-Monopolist Traditions,"** *The Nation* (February 3, 2020)

WOLFF, Richard D., *Democracy at Work: A Cure for Capitalism* (Chicago, IL: Haymarket Books, 2012)

WOLFF, Richard D, *The Sickness is the System: When Capitalism Fails to Save Us from the Pandemic or Itself* (NY: Democracy at Work, 2020)

WOLIN, Sheldon S, *Democracy Incorporated: Managed Democracy and the Specter of Inverted Totalitarianism* (Princeton, NJ: Princeton University Press, 2008)

ZELIZER, Julian E, ***Burning Down the House: Newt Gingrich and the Rise of the New Republican Party*** (NY: Penguin Bood, 2020)

ZINN, Howard, ***A People's History of the United States, 1492-2001*** (NY: Harper Co

Liberty and Justice For All